WHAT IF YOU'RE DOING IT RIGHT?

31 DAYS TO UNCOVERING THE CONFIDENCE AND
HAPPINESS YOU DESERVE

ROBIN BRANDE

RYER PUBLISHING

WHAT IF YOU'RE DOING IT RIGHT?
31 Days To Uncovering the Confidence and Happiness You Deserve

By Robin Brande

Published by Ryer Publishing
www.ryerpublishing.com
Copyright 2018 by Robin Brande
www.robinbrande.com
Cover art by Katerina Sisperova/Dreamstime
Cover design by Ryer Publishing

All rights reserved.

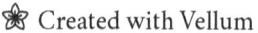

ALSO BY ROBIN BRANDE

Dove Season-Series

Dove Season

Finder

Seeker

Believer

Winnie-Parsons-Mysteries

The Genius Track

A Man of Appetites

A Drop of Sweat

The Long Gray Hook

The Slip of a Rib

Collections

The Love of a Good Dog

Mountain Tough

Bradamante-Saga

Book of Earth

Book of Water

Parallelogram-Series

Into the Parallel

Caught in the Parallel

Seize the Parallel

Beyond the Parallel

Young-Adult

Evolution, Me & Other Freaks of Nature

Fat Cat

Doggirl

Replay

Romance

Love Proof

Right On Time

Freefall

Heart of Ice

Fire and Ice

Self-Help

What If You're Doing It Right?

What If You're Doing It Right? For Teens

WHAT IF YOU'RE DOING IT RIGHT?

CONTENTS

Introduction	ix
1. What if you get to decide how you want your life to be?	1
2. What if the world needs your particular Uses?	5
3. What if you begin again each morning?	11
4. What if you don't need permission?	15
5. What if you don't need advice?	21
6. What if you already hold the answers that you need?	25
7. What if you design your life to fit you, not someone else?	31
8. What if you give up caring what other people think of your plans?	35
9. What if your body is already right?	41
10. What if you always wear clothing that fits?	47
11. What if you're not in trouble?	51
12. What if you are the special occasion?	55
13. What if you get to flourish?	59
14. What if you take secret delight in your many talents?	65
15. What if you teach people how to treat you?	69
16. What if you accept people's kindness?	73
17. What if you're allowed to learn as much as you want to?	79
18. What if you can do as many occupations as you want?	83
19. What if you put yourself first?	89
20. What if saying no can feel as comfortable as saying yes?	95
21. What if failure is only a temporary condition?	99

22. What if you simply apologize to yourself and
    move on? 103
23. What if making changes is easier than you
    think? 107
24. What if your time is for you? 113
25. What if your money is for you? 119
26. What if you want to pursue your dream? 127
27. What if you're not too late? 131
28. What if you aim past your targets? 137
29. What if not sharing who you are deprives the
    world of a gift? 141
30. What if you're ready to go for it? 145
31. What if you're doing it right? 151

About the Author 155

INTRODUCTION

I am over fifty years old now, and one day I realized that meant I had spent nearly fifty years worrying that I wasn't doing it right. Whatever "it" was.

My career, my appearance, my personal life, my professional life, my writing, my exercise, my behavior, my attitude, my my my…

Fifty years is a lot of time to waste on feeling wrong.

Fifty *minutes* is too long.

So what's changed now?

I finally started putting into play the wide variety of lessons I've learned over the years as a martial artist, lawyer, teacher, student, seeker, finder, and trier.

And now I want you to have the benefit of those same lessons. It's like stepping onto the moving sidewalk in an airport. I'm happy to help you reach the destination of finding your own happiness and personal strength without having to take as long as I did.

You'll find that a lot of this book is about skipping steps. Maybe you've convinced yourself that making certain changes in your life will take a very long time. What if it won't? What if the most stubborn barriers in your life can disappear in an instant?

You're going to find out how.

But first, let's make sure we're beginning on the same page:

What if you're doing it right? Whatever "it" is.

What if your spontaneous ideas about how to live and what to do are **correct**, and you stopped trying to talk yourself out of them?

What would a whole day look like if you knew that everything you did was right? How you dressed, how you ate, how you acted, how you thought—**what would that day feel like?**

What if you changed your focus away from how other people are doing their lives, and instead asked yourself, **"What are my Uses in this world?"** What if spending the rest of your life joyfully pursuing and fulfilling your Uses is the most important thing you ever have to do anymore?

What if instead of asking yourself, "What should I be doing with my life?" instead you asked, **"How do I want my life to be?"**

How much bravery would that take?

And what if you're already that brave, and you just don't know it?

It's like those movies where the bad guys have launched their attack, all seems lost, and then suddenly the humble, ordinary shopkeeper turns out to have amazing martial arts skills. There was no need to show that before or brag about it, but when the time came and those skills were needed—GO.

Maybe that's where you are in your life right now. The time has come and your skills are needed.

GO.

1

WHAT IF YOU GET TO DECIDE HOW YOU WANT YOUR LIFE TO BE?

Sometimes it takes a dramatic event to shake us off a path that is no longer right for us.

My friend Anna is one of the toughest, coolest women I know. I met her several years ago when we practiced martial arts together. She was studying for her PhD in Pharmacology and Toxicology at the time. She had gone straight through school, always knew she would be a scientist (her family knew it, too, and were very proud of her for that), and she had her PhD dissertation topic already picked out. She worked for one of her professors in a lab doing fascinating, important research.

Despite the intense demands of her studies, she also had an active physical life. In addition to training in martial arts she played on a rugby team, ran, hiked, biked, skied, snowboarded, kayaked—the list went on and on. She loved being outdoors and loved using her body. She was then and still is my definition of *burly*.

Then one day on the drive home from an out-of-state rugby game, the car Anna was riding in was involved in a serious accident. Everyone lived, but Anna's pelvis was shattered and she couldn't walk for over a year. She was bed-bound for the first three months, then in a wheelchair for the next twelve.

As she lay there in the hospital, unable to move for the next few months, she had nothing but time to think. And what she realized was that she had completely lost interest in pursing her PhD any longer. She was over it. She had been on this track all of her life, but now … no. She thought about how her boss at the lab loved her job so much she would often fall asleep on the lab table. Anna didn't feel that way about her lab work. She knew it was not her passion after all.

And here's why Anna's story, for all its inspiring details about her grit and perseverance in making a complete comeback (not only did she walk again, but she was back to playing rugby within two years), made such an impact on me when I heard it. Instead of asking herself, "What do I want to do now?" or "What do I want to be?" she asked, **"How do I want my life to be?"**

She spent the entire fifteen months of her recovery exploring her answers to that question. She was in no rush to figure everything out. This was her life. Her family wasn't happy she was quitting science, but she couldn't muster even a pretend desire for it anymore. That version of her life was over.

She thought about all of the elements that she wanted to include from now on: outdoor sports, travel, fun, being among people instead of being stuck in a research lab. She considered going to medical school, but didn't want to be in the same situation of spending a lot of years at something and then discovering that she didn't like it after all. So instead she went into Emergency Medical Technician training, since it involved only one semester of course work (well within her science capability) to become certified.

She loved the work. She loved saving people. She loved working with her fellow EMTs. It was enough of a test run to convince her that she would be happy taking the next step and becoming a nurse.

Now she's what's known as a travel nurse. She works thirteen weeks at a time in various locations all around the country. It allows her to pursue her passion of helping people, while also including the other elements on her list: seeing new places, meeting new people, and trying new outdoor sports in every new location. Through a series of unlikely and at times unfortunate events, she has designed exactly the right life for herself.

Could she have done excellent work in this world if she had remained on her PhD track and become a research scientist? I have no doubt. But even if she had left the scientific field entirely, Anna would have added value—high value—to everyone she met no matter what career she ultimately chose. Her upbeat, adventurous, burly approach to life can't help but inspire the people around her to step up their own games.

As we explore in the coming chapters the various ways to tailor your own life to fit you—specifically *you*—think about your own answer to Anna's wonderful question: **How do I want my life to be?** The elements you identify for your own list can make all the difference to your happiness and satisfaction—not to mention the ways you choose to use your talents in the world.

- Spend time today asking yourself some of Anna's questions:

- How do you want your daily life to be?
- If you could choose from scratch, where would you like to live? Do you prefer someplace rural or in the city?
- What kinds of physical activities do you enjoy? Is being outdoors important to you?
- Would you rather work around other people, or alone? Would you rather work with animals or people?
- What type of work sounds fulfilling, even if it's not what you're studying for or doing now? Do you want a job where you're helping people, or does that honestly not match your personality?

2

WHAT IF THE WORLD NEEDS YOUR PARTICULAR USES?

The capitalization of Uses is my own, because I think there's a difference between all the things we *can* do and all the things we're really *here* to do—the things that make us feel cheerful and fulfilled and, well, of use.

Some of us *can* play the piano or create intricate spreadsheets or run heavy machinery or run fast, and if you sat down and made a list of all the many things you can do, you could probably keep writing for a long time.

But just because you can do all those many things, does it mean that those skills and talents are (a) what you most delight in sharing, and (b) what the world needs from you?

I remember an example in a career guidance book I once read: The writer who uses his talents to create deodorant ads might enjoy his work, but does the world really need that from him? Maybe he has wisdom or humor to share, and we would all be so much better off if he would finally gather up his courage to direct his efforts there and we could read what he has to say.

Conversely, the doctor who is out in the field curing some horrible contagious disease is doing work that the world needs, but if she hates her job every single day, is that the right place for her? Maybe she's keeping some other person from taking the job, and that person would continue the work and take great joy and satisfaction from doing it.

In other words, we can't really know, can we? What each person does with his or her life is very personal to them. What you choose to do is personal to you. Which means—and here's the good news—it is absolutely right for you to be the one to decide.

So think about it in terms of your Uses: those things that you are skilled at doing and that you enjoy doing most. Sit down and make that list for yourself. It can tell you a lot.

Not everything will seem important to other people. Who cares? It's not their list. My own list contains plenty of outwardly useful things like writing, teaching, and providing both legal and minor medical advice if either are needed, but it also includes things like being a good dog mom and a good baker; cheerfully cleaning my house because I enjoy the way it looks afterward; and knowing how to help the college students in my family write better essays and research papers because I geek out on things like that. It's a way I can help and I love it.

On the other hand, I could run for public office, go back to practicing law, or write textbooks. I have the education and ability to do all three, and the world might need them done, but not by me. I wouldn't enjoy them. Those are not my Uses, they are someone else's.

Whereas writing this book does feel like one of my Uses. I had the idea and decided to follow through.

Does all of this mean that you should quit your unfulfilling job today so you can go volunteer at the animal shelter or finally sit down and write your novel? Not necessarily. (And by the way, life still goes on while you're writing a novel. You'll still want to pay your bills and keep up with the laundry.) This might not be the right time for a dramatic change yet because one of your current Users might be to earn enough money to pay the rent or mortgage and otherwise support yourself and your family. But you might now have an incentive to explore which money earning jobs would be a better fit while you continue to lay your own path toward fulfillment.

Uses don't always have to be active. The innate qualities of your personality are also what you have to offer. I saw a demonstration of this recently when my wonderful father-in-law died at the age of 95. By then he had been suffering from dementia and various physical ailments for several years. He lived much longer than any of his doctors expected. It didn't seem to be a good life by the end. He was reduced to living in one room, being moved between his bed and his favorite chair. He couldn't enjoy his food anymore. His once happy and fulfilling life now seemed very small and sad.

I had a conversation with his hospice nurse about how someone in his condition could continue to survive. She said that some people just kept hanging on for reasons we might never know.

It wasn't until after he finally died that I learned about what Use he was still fulfilling, even in those last years. He was a cheerful, positive man, both before and after the dementia. Many of the care workers told me that he was the patient who made their days better because he was always so pleasant and grateful. That was his nature. One of the hospice nurses told me that she always scheduled her visits to him at the end of her rounds so she could end her day with a smile. Even then my father-in-law was making people's lives better in his own personal way. It was one of his Uses.

Are you kind? Are you honest? Those are among your Uses in this world. We often discount the value of being a good person—simply that, a good person—when it actually matters a lot in a world where not everyone is good. Think about all the many qualities you have to offer. Not every Use is tangible or splashy or noticeable by others. But *you* know. And as we'll discuss later, taking secret delight in your own competence and good deeds is often reward enough.

So as you go about your life today, start paying attention to the things you do and *like* doing. Notice all the things you're good at, whether they seem "important enough" or not. Notice when some aspect of your personality shines through, like when you offer encouragement to a co-worker or give a genuine smile and thank you to the person who hands you your coffee. All of these things are among your Uses.

Also notice which things are clearly **not** your Uses. When you watch a snippet of news, you might know that being a politician is not your Use. If crying babies jangle your nerves, then working with babies and small children probably isn't your Use. You can appreciate that someone is doing a particular type of work in this world without thinking you have to do that work, too. I, personally, wouldn't do well as a first grade teacher or a policewoman. But I'm so grateful that some people do those careers. Those are their Uses, not mine.

All of this is good information to help you direct your path. There are no right or wrong answers—this is all absolutely personal to you. Thinking about your Uses will help you identify all of the best ways to spend your time and efforts and life going forward.

- Today pay attention throughout the day to when you know you have performed one of your Uses. Stop and consider how that feels. Do the same when you have done something that does not feel like your Use.

- Begin honing your activities, roles, and behaviors to more closely match what you know your Uses are.

3

WHAT IF YOU BEGIN AGAIN EACH MORNING?

Every day is a fresh chance to begin again. Actually, every minute offers a fresh chance, but let's begin with days.

Nature has a way of cleaning the slate every single night. The sun goes down, bringing a natural end to the day that was, whether it was good or bad, and with the sunrise every morning we have the chance to begin again. To start fresh.

Some people feel the need to wait for some special event on the calendar to change how they manage their lives. New Year's Day is a popular one, as are birthdays, anniversaries, back-to-school, and other occasions.

But why wait? Every day is yours. Every hour and minute are yours. If you feel that you have been leading your life in a direction that no longer appeals to you, stop now and reassess. You haven't "ruined" things, it's not too late, you can choose to reset at any moment.

There is a concept in the ancient Chinese text the *I Ching* that if you feel you have made a mistake of some kind, all you have to do is get right back on your "superior path." It's a wonderful image. Maybe you've spent days or years walking in a ditch or through the brambles, when finally you realize this isn't where you want to be anymore. It's not too late—never, while you're still alive. All you have to do is turn to the side, lift up one foot and then the other, and immediately step back on to your superior path. Then you can continue on the way you prefer to go.

Were you sad yesterday? Angry? Pitiful and hurt? Did you make mistakes and feel foolish or betrayed? Were you the one who hurt or betrayed someone else? Did you fall short in some way that you regret?

Not today. Today is new. You are new. You decide who you are and how you feel. No one stands between you and the person you prefer to be. Take control of your life. Be in charge of your mood. Your emotions and your behavior belong to you, no one else. You decide.

Let your body help you. Stand up tall. Look into your own eyes in the mirror. Smile at yourself. Give yourself some words of encouragement: "I love you. You're kind. You're smart. You're strong. I'm proud of you." Who wouldn't want to start every day hearing that?

And if you have made some mistake that left you cringing and wishing you could go back and undo it, realize two things: No, you haven't "ruined everything," but also, you're not off the hook. Get back to doing what you know is best for you, and don't delay a single second.

Those of us who have been chronic dieters during our lives know exactly what this looks like: *I already blew my diet by eating this cookie, so I might as well eat the whole dozen.*

But it also applies to any setback, whether it's self-created or some obstacle imposed from outside. Sometimes it seems so much easier to stop where we are, stop trying, and just blame it on the roadblock … forgetting or ignoring that we can go around it, over it, under it, call in a crew of our friends to help us blast through it—the remedy varies.

It's why reminding ourselves of our goals and our ideal versions of ourselves is so important. And it's important to do often. Because setbacks *will* come, our own fortitude *will* waver, and whether or not we ultimately succeed rests with our attitude toward ourselves.

Do you believe in your heart you are meant for and capable of great things? Do you have faith in your own good? If so, shake off your mistakes or outside difficulties, take a fresh breath, and go ahead and get right back on the path you mean to walk. You are in charge of your own future. Be brave and persistent on your own behalf.

And there's no time like right now to fix things. Shake off the past. Get that sharp image in your mind once more of who you want to be.

Then off you go. Onward. Keep faith in your heart, in your talents, and in your passion for doing what you want. Every day is a fresh chance to start over, and at any moment in your life you can make an adjustment to your course and get back to your own superior path.

Seize each new day. Step by step by step.

- Today start fresh. And if it's already midday or evening, start fresh again. Every new minute really is a chance to clear the slate, shake off the past, and go forward in the way your prefer. Start thinking of your time as infinitely refreshing itself. Begin again as many times as you need all day, every day.

- Is there some new habit you can add to your mornings to emphasize that you're starting over again, just like the new day? It might be spending a minute or two in bed before you leap out, and thinking about how you'd like the day to go. Sometimes our way of rushing into the day as if we're already late for our lives can rob us of the chance to make decisions of our own about how we'd like things to be. Take the time. Give it to yourself. Just five minutes of quiet and thoughtfulness every morning can make a huge difference in your feelings about the day.

4

WHAT IF YOU DON'T NEED PERMISSION?

Are you still waiting for someone else's permission before you feel you're allowed to live your life the way you intend? What if the only permission you ever need is your own? Would that eliminate any artificial waiting period that's holding you back?

Seasoned lawyers and judges love to play tricks on new young lawyers. Ha-ha, it's so funny—unless you're the young lawyer.

It was my first year as an associate, and my first time ever in bankruptcy court, covering a hearing for one of the partners in my firm. I had prepared for days ahead of time, knew what my argument was going to be, had worn my lucky suit—I was ready.

When the case was called, I got up with the opposing attorney and took my place at the front of the courtroom, and when I announced my name and was ready to launch into my prepared speech, the judge stopped me.

"Have you been admitted to bankruptcy court?"

Panic sweat. I was admitted to the Bar, but I didn't realize there was a special step I had to go through to be admitted to the bankruptcy division of the Bar. My boss hadn't told me! I didn't know what to do.

"Uh ... no, your Honor. I haven't." I was going to have to go back to the office and confess I'd completely botched the hearing. I felt stupid and humiliated.

The judge pointed to one of the old warhorses of the bankruptcy division, a lawyer who had been one of my law professors—a scary one, at that—and told him, "Admit her."

That lawyer stood, walked up to where I waited with my knees wobbling from the stress, and made the motion of the cross in front of me.

"There," the judge said, "you're admitted."

Howls of laughter from all the other lawyers waiting around for their own cases to be called. I smiled feebly. Then tried to gather my courage and what little confidence remained so that I could actually go through with the hearing.

While secretly seething.

Needless to say, I HATE stuff like that. It's mean and unnecessary and an abuse of power and authority. I would never do that to a fellow human—especially someone just starting out in a profession that's already stressful enough—and I doubt you would, either. But that's not the point of the story.

The point is, there might be things in your life right now that you're waiting for permission to do, but that permission is as artificial as the swearing in I received. Do you think there's some step that you have to master or someone's approval you have to gain before you qualify to become the person you intend to be?

A former colleague of mine recently quit practicing law (probably because it's so mean) and started her own web-based business based on one of the hobbies she's always been passionate about. She has a lot of great, useful information to share with people just like her, and she's eager to share it.

Except...

"Do you know how many other people there are who know how to do the same things I'm doing?" she said. "There are so many other websites and blogs. What makes me an expert? Why should people listen to me?"

I told her three reasons:

1. She's actually doing the thing she's talking about, out there having the experiences, not just reading about them or theorizing;

2. She's willing to be thoughtful about them. Willing to actually analyze what does and doesn't work, what she can do to make it better and easier, and how she can teach those skills to others; and

3. She's willing to put herself out there and write about it. To put in the effort to organize the information and curate resources from other places so that anyone coming

to her site has a one-stop place to learn what they need to know.

"That's what makes you an expert," I said. "And so what if there are a hundred other people out there with their own websites talking about their own opinions of how to do it right? The people who want their take on it will go there. The people who like what you have to say will come to you."

And in my mind, I gave her the Bankruptcy Cross: *There. You're admitted.*

If you've been feeling the same kind of hesitation, be willing to believe that the only credential you need—the only permission—is your own talent and desire to pursue what you have in mind. You might need real certifications along the way, or degrees or licenses, but for right now, to get started, to take that first step toward who you want to be and what you want to do—

All you need is your own permission. Stand in front of the mirror and admit yourself to whatever group or profession or big juicy life you've been wanting to pursue. You don't have to wait for *anybody* to say it's okay. You get to decide in your heart who you are and what is meaningful to you in your life, and then begin mapping out how to get there.

Don't wait for someone else to tell you it's okay. Don't wait until you feel like an expert or worry whether people will wonder what makes *you* so special that you think you can do this. You're already there. You are that special. So stand up and own it and go for it.

- Today ask yourself what you've been waiting for permission to do. It might be pursuing a certain job or hobby, or you might just want to learn something new that you've been curious about for a while. Have you always wanted to learn how to play the guitar? Do you wish you could knit or do woodworking or build your own website? You don't have to justify how any of those things might lead to income or prestige or anything tangible at all. You can learn and do things simply for your own satisfaction. So go ahead and give yourself permission. You're allowed to live a full and interesting life.

5

WHAT IF YOU DON'T NEED ADVICE?

Sometimes we ask for advice while knowing full well that we don't need it. We might want confirmation of something we've already decided, but that's different. That's lack of confidence, not lack of knowledge.

Asking for advice is an effective delay tactic to keep us from beginning whatever it is we say we want to begin. For writers it often takes the form of needing to do more research before we can begin a book. Do we really? Or could we begin writing now and look up applicable information as we go? Once the manuscript is finished, we can delay publication—and public exposure—even longer by sending it around to other writer friends asking for their input and advice. And if the answers that come back conflict with each other—"Chapter 3 is too slow." "Chapter 3 was my favorite!"—then it means another round of rewrites trying to make everyone else happy.

While meanwhile the world of readers can't lay eyes on anything new that you've created because you're too busy rewriting it to death.

There can be the same insecurity and procrastination with people thinking of starting their own businesses. It's smart to ask other business owners and entrepreneurs how they got started and what they wish they had known ahead of time or done differently, but after that initial due diligence, it might be better to get going and start small, rather than keep putting it off because you think you have to start big.

A woman I met recently who owns her own retail business selling specialty food items for gourmet cooks seems to be on the fast track to success. She opened her shop only a year ago, and already she has a thriving both online and storefront presence. In addition, she's written and published her own guide to the various ingredients that she sells. The book includes scientific information, food lore, and recipes. She's already sold over a hundred copies.

How did she get so much confidence? Why did she think she could do everything she's done so far, and in such a short amount of time?

"I didn't ask anybody," she told me. "I just did it. I'm sure everybody would have told me I was crazy to try half of the things I have. That's why I just did it before anyone talked me out of it."

Notice your own behavior. Start paying attention to how often you ask people for advice, but don't really mean it. It might be something small, like asking whether a new movie is good, when you've already decided to see it anyway.

Or it might be something larger, like asking for career advice when your heart is already pulling you in a particular direction. If the answer the person gives is different from your own desire, now you have another layer of obligation, thinking you might disappoint the advisor by ignoring his or her guidance.

Skip the pretend appeal for help. The more you listen to your own opinions and try what you think is right for you, the more confidence you'll build in yourself. If you try something and it doesn't work, that's good information for you. If you try and you succeed, take the next logical step.

No one is born with a roadmap laying out every infallible step of their lives. We all learn as we go. And learning for yourself when you already have a good idea what you want to do gives you the kind of strength and self-assurance that you won't gain if you always depend on others to lead you.

- Today notice any time you ask someone their opinion when you don't actually care. You might be just trying to make conversation—"How is it out there? Hot?"—or you might realize that you habitually ask people for advice when you don't truly need it.

- Notice, then stop. You might even have to stop mid-sentence, but that's better than unconsciously continuing the habit. Start asking yourself questions instead. What do *you* think about this? What would *you* do in this situation? What would you tell someone else if they came to you and asked the same question that you were about to pose to someone else? If anyone you know has ever asked you for advice, then you know you're qualified to offer it to yourself, too.

- Is there something you've been waiting to do, but you feel the need to pass it by a few other people first? What if you just moved ahead confidently without waiting for their input? If not the whole entire project, is there at least a smaller part of it that you can go ahead and release into the world before everyone else says it's good? One way we build confidence in our abilities and our judgment is by trying things even when we're not completely certain. Be willing to move forward with an idea that you have, trusting that you can rely on your own internal advice.

6

WHAT IF YOU ALREADY HOLD THE ANSWERS THAT YOU NEED?

Write to yourself. Ask yourself questions out loud. Both of these are the simplest and yet most powerful tools you have at your disposal for uncovering how you really want to live your life and how you want to be.

Sometimes we don't truly know how we feel about something or what we think about a particular issue until we see it in our own handwriting on a page. It's why love letters can be so powerful: The writer has taken the time and care to express his or her feelings in words beyond just "I love you" (although those are good words, too). When we take the time and care to talk to ourselves in writing, even if it's only for fifteen minutes a day, those fifteen minutes might be our best way of finding out what we're really thinking and feeling about our lives. And the more we understand that, the better we are at mapping out where we want to go next and what we want to do.

I prefer to write to myself on plain, loose leaf notebook paper. Those fancy, bound journals make me feel too much pressure to write something Literary and Important. Notebook paper feels casual and uncomplicated. And if what I write to myself on a particular day is so personal and petty and unflattering that I would hate for my husband or anyone else to find it, it's easy to feed those pages into the shredder as soon as I'm done. The value of this tool is in the process of communicating with yourself honestly and freely—not in keeping what you've written.

What to write? It might be as simple as a list of things to do or your thoughts about the upcoming events of the day. You might write to yourself about some issue you're having with a person in your life. You might finally write down some of the creative ideas you've been mulling over. It doesn't matter what you write, what matters is the habit. Because over time you will feel more and more comfortable expressing to yourself whatever is on your mind.

These pages are for you. They are a chance to sit down with yourself and have a conversation when you're giving yourself your own complete attention. There are no rules about how to do them right.

Sometimes I start my pages with a simple greeting: "Hi! Here's what's going on." Then I take it from there and just have a nice handwritten chat. I love it. I'm my own friend. I always appreciate it when I spend that little bit of quiet time with myself.

If taking time to write to yourself every day feels unrealistic because of your schedule and obligations, don't give up. There's another easy way of holding a conversation with yourself to find out what's on your mind.

How often do you talk to yourself? All day long? Never? Somewhere in between? In the same way we don't always know what we think or how we feel until we see it in our own handwriting on a page, we might not know what is truly going on in our lives unless someone takes the trouble to ask.

It's no trouble. We can do it ourselves.

People rarely ask us how we feel. Even your close friends or family probably don't take the time throughout every day to check in and see how you are. At least not to this extent:

"How do you feel right now?"

Tired.

"What do you need?"

I don't know. Maybe some food. Maybe a break.

"What kind of food?"

I don't know.

"But if you did know, what would it be?"

Okay, probably a banana.

"Then let's go get that."

And so on.

It might seem like a trivial conversation, but it's part of an important overall practice of giving yourself your own time and attention.

It's so easy to gloss over our own feelings during the

busy-ness of the day. We just keep doing and going and never take a moment to find out what we think and how we feel about everything that's going on. But it's so easy to take that moment.

Try talking to yourself out loud. You can ask yourself questions in the privacy of your shower or as you wait for your coffee to brew. Talk quietly to yourself while you walk somewhere or while driving alone in your car. If you're worried about what it looks like, know that in this age of mobile phone earpieces people will assume you're talking to someone else.

Ask follow up questions any time you're tempted to answer with less than the full, deep truth.

"You seem a little glum right now. Why?"

I don't know.

"Well, if you did know, why would that be?"

There's something magical about that last question. Often we really *do* know the answer to why we think or feel a certain way, but we've gotten into the habit over the years of shrugging and moving on. That might work with outsiders, but not with someone who knows you as well as you do. So keep asking until you find out exactly what's on your mind. It's a relief to be able to share it. You're doing yourself a favor.

You might realize how many times you turn to your television or computer for entertainment, when talking to yourself for a few minutes instead might turn out to be a much more relaxing break.

Even if you don't have a specific topic to address, there

are always questions you can enjoy asking yourself every day, in part because it's so nice that someone finally wants to know:

"How are you feeling right now? What can I get you? What would make you happy right now? What are you looking forward to today? What are you worried about? What else do you want to tell me?"

Who wouldn't want to live each day with that kind of loving attention? Start now and give it to yourself.

- Today buy a package of loose leaf notebook paper. Then spend at least fifteen minutes this evening or whenever you can be alone and quiet, and start a conversation with yourself on paper. It can begin as easily as, "Hi! Here I am. What do you want to say?" Try writing quickly and continuously for the full fifteen minutes. You might go longer some days, shorter others. It doesn't matter. What matters is the daily habit. The more comfortable you become seeing what you have to say in your own handwriting, the easier it will be to find out how you truly feel and what you want from your life each day. You'll see other places in this book where writing to yourself is the perfect tool.

- As you walk or drive somewhere or stand in the shower, start asking yourself questions: "How do you feel right now? Are you enjoying your day? Can I get you anything to make you feel better? Are you hungry? What food do you want me to give you?" Just ask. And listen. Get used to caring what's on your own mind. Creating the habit of asking yourself questions builds trust and confidence between the busy, active, outside you and the quieter, thoughtful, deep-feeling version inside. You'll also find places in this book where asking yourself questions will help you uncover the answers that you need.

7

WHAT IF YOU DESIGN YOUR LIFE TO FIT YOU, NOT SOMEONE ELSE?

Look around you at your home, your clothes, your job, your social circle, your daily activities: Do they suit you? Do they match your personality and what you like? Or are they someone else's idea of the best way you should live?

Years ago I read a product review in an outdoor sports magazine that became the perfect metaphor for this. The reviewer laid out all the great features of some of the newest 4-season tents—the kind you can use in the summer heat of Baja and still be comfortable in during winter snows in Alaska—but then the reviewer added some philosophy at the end:

"Ask yourself, *do* I really camp out all year long? Or do I just think I might want to some day? In which case, wouldn't it make more sense to spend less money on a 3-

season tent now, and then upgrade only if and when you really need more?"

Wow, did that change my life.

Because that 3-season tent test turns out to apply to so many different things, once you really start examining your life.

Take your living situation: Maybe most of the people you know think that owning a home is the ultimate goal, but is that honestly what's right for you? Or do you prefer the flexibility of renting so you can move any time you want?

Maybe some people think having a four-bedroom house is the best, but do you? Or do you just want a two-bedroom because those are the only rooms you actually need?

And think about your clothes: Maybe you have a closet full of outfits you bought at one time thinking you'd definitely wear them, but as you live your life day to day, you really keep returning to the same few comfortable pairs of pants and your favorite four or five shirts. Does it make sense to keep storing all those extra clothes, when someone else could be enjoying them right now if you just cleared them out and gave them away?

And what about how you've decorated your space? Maybe other people think you've gone too far with your stuffed animals or your litter boxes in every room or some of the artwork you have on your walls, but do those things make *you* happy? Isn't that the test?

A friend of mine came over the other day and used our

guest bathroom and came out shaking her head. I didn't even have to ask her why: She's super chic, and we recently redecorated our bathroom to include one of the cheesiest shower curtains I've ever seen. It looks like something you'd find in a 1950s grandmother's home: old-fashioned colors and a repeating pattern of deer, bears, and canoes. Why did I buy it? Because I wanted my bathroom to remind me of a cabin where I stayed last summer. It makes me happy. I'm allowed to have a shower curtain that makes me happy.

Would my sophisticated friend ever dream of putting something like that in her own home? Not even on a dare. But she might visit my bathroom only once a year, whereas I go in there every day. So I get to choose.

When you make choices about what to buy and how to live based on how some other person would do it, you're falling for the 4-season tent. You think you *might* turn into that other kind of person some day, so you'd better be prepared.

But what if who you are right now is already the real you? And why isn't that enough? You like the things you like. You live the way you enjoy. Your natural personality and preferences have been steering you all along to make the choices that work for you. And it's time to stop apologizing for that.

Be yourself today. Have and wear and do the things that make *you* happy—even if they wouldn't be right for someone else. Who cares what they like? You're here to live *your* life. Your 3-season tent is *perfect*.

- Today look around your home and notice all the things in it that really are *you*. They might be decorative items or pieces of furniture or the special coffee mugs you collect from your trips. Notice which items bring up some happy association: maybe you bought it for yourself as a treat, someone you love gave it to you, or it's something sentimental that you've kept for years.

- Now notice all the things you've surrounded yourself with that don't really fit who you are. Were they gifts that you feel you still have to keep and display? Were they things you purchased some time ago when your interests were different—or *you* were different? We all go through periods of trying to figure out who we are. There's no shame in realizing that you're still holding on to artifacts that no longer suit you.

- Start honing your possessions. Decide which ones you would actually be relieved to see go. Sell, give, donate. Know that you've already gotten your full use out of these things—even if you've only had them a short while—and cheerfully move them on to new owners who can enjoy them for a full fresh run of time.

8

WHAT IF YOU GIVE UP CARING WHAT OTHER PEOPLE THINK OF YOUR PLANS?

How different would it feel to give up caring what other people think about your plans? It might require a radical shift in thinking, but the relief and freedom are worth it.

After law school my friend Christine took a job with a prestigious law firm in Chicago. For several years she loved the pace and the challenge of the work, but after a decade in the job she realized it was wearing her down. The hours were too long, the pressure was intense, and she had lost all of her passion for the law. She knew in her heart it was time to make a change. But a change to what?

She had saved some money, intending to buy a condominium at some point, but now she realized that money gave her a certain amount of freedom. She decided to use it to give herself the gift of time. Much to the shock of her friends and co-workers, she quit her job without having another one to take its place. Christine had something else in mind.

For the past several months as she stared out the window of the downtown high rise where she worked, she had been fantasizing about what it would be like to live in the country. Sometimes when she needed a break from writing endless legal papers, she would browse through property listings on real estate websites.

Eventually she saw something that made her heart leap. It was a pretty, one-bedroom cottage in a small town in the Colorado mountains. It seemed like the perfect place to spend a year figuring out her life. So after quitting her job she rented out her Chicago apartment to someone else and leased the pretty little cottage for a year.

Not a single one of her Chicago friends supported her decision. Her family took it better, but even they seemed skeptical that she could manage in such a different place. People acted as though she were moving to the untamed frontier.

And it was an adjustment, but exactly the one she wanted. Suddenly her days were wide open. She refused to have a schedule. She loved the much slower pace of the town, the people, even the slower speed limits on the roadways. She spent her days hiking, reading, taking art classes, and learning new country skills like how to make jam and can her own fruits and vegetables in season.

It was her fantasy come true. And she found that it suited her better than she ever could have imagined.

After a few months of doing nothing but exactly what

she wanted, she started thinking about whether she wanted to live there permanently. If so, she would need work of some kind. This year of play was wonderful, but it wouldn't last forever.

People in the community seemed to patch together all sorts of work for themselves: part-time baker, part-time babysitter, part-time cook and construction worker in the summer and ski instructor in the winter. For the first time in her life Christine saw that she didn't have to be only one thing. (We'll talk about that more in Chapter 18.)

She knew she had valuable skills as a lawyer and a legal writer. Neither appealed to her anymore, but she wondered if she could apply those skills to something that had also been in the back of her mind for some time.

She started spending part of every day writing her first legal thriller. She still had another half year of savings to live on, so she felt no pressure to earn any income from book sales to support herself, she just wanted to see if she could do it.

And yes, she could. Very well, in fact. She sent me an early draft and I loved it.

Now she's lived in her pretty little cottage in the mountains for over three years. There have been challenges, of course, but overall, she says, it was the best change she could have made.

Still, every now and then she would hear from her former friends and colleagues, and no matter how many positive things she tried to tell them about her new life, they acted as though she had made a mistake. She could be a partner in the law firm by now. She could be earning more than ever before. "You're writing now? How much money does *that* make?"

One day, after hanging up the phone after another conversation like that and feeling the familiar deflation of her mood that followed, she suddenly realized she didn't have to feel that way ever again. First, she might stop answering those calls altogether: they always made her feel bad, and she never gained anything of value from them.

But second, even if she ever did have to hear from the people in her former life that she was wasting her time, that she should return to her "real" life and she could still vacation in the mountains if she wanted and even "afford to stay someplace much nicer" (that one made her blood hot), Christine realized there was only one right answer to all of them, even if she only said it in her head:

"You don't even know what I'm doing, so why should I care what you think?"

Has she actually said that out loud to anyone? One person, but Christine said he just laughed and kept telling her why she was wrong. That was the last phone call she took from him. And she secretly made him the villain in her next book.

You, too, might find yourself subject to criticism as you shed more and more layers on your way to uncovering your authentic life. People around you might still want to hold you to standards that no longer apply.

Consider keeping Christine's phrase always at the ready in your mind: "You don't even know what I'm doing, so why should I care what you think?" Saying it out loud might feel rude in certain circumstances, but saying it to yourself can be just what you need to bring your blood pressure down and keep a cheerful feeling in your heart.

Seeing someone change and make new choices can make the people around us feel uncomfortable and even threatened. Everyone feels safe with the familiar. But their discomfort is not a reason for you to halt your own progress toward a life that suits you better. They'll catch up. Or not. In the meantime, on you go.

- Today think about some of the elements of your current life. Do you still like your work or what you're pursuing in school? Do you like the area where you live? Are you secretly longing to change your living situation in a major way? Do you want to move to the city or someplace rural, or to an entirely different country than where you live now?

- Ask yourself questions about it. Write to yourself and see what you think. Put some of your ideas onto paper where you can see them and start considering what you truly want.

- As with every new direction we want to pursue, there are always specific steps that we can take. What are yours? Can you begin with the first and easiest steps right away? Even spending time researching a new place or a new career might be exactly what you need right now to appease any restlessness you're feeling. You might discover that the idea you have isn't as great as you thought. Or you might receive further confirmation that it's the direction you want to take. Find out. Knowledge is good.

9

WHAT IF YOUR BODY IS ALREADY RIGHT?

Do you ever feel as if you're at war with your own body? Do you constantly criticize it in your own mind, or even out loud, maybe under some misguided belief that your disapproval will somehow motivate you to make a change in how you eat or exercise or generally live?

What if you just stopped all that? What if you skipped the self-cruelty, and simply lived on a daily basis in a way that felt friendly to your own body and its health?

One of the things I've apologized to myself for (see Chapter 22) was all of the dieting I forced myself to do from when I was about 11 years old until my late 40s. That's a very long time to be disappointed in my body. I'm so sad that I did that to myself. The dieting wasn't constant, but the thoughts behind it were. I traded back and forth between being a tyrant to myself and the rebel who resisted. *"No more cookies!" "All the cookies!"*

We had a lot to fight over, myself and I, until I finally got it out of my system by writing about an overweight teen in my novel *Fat Cat*. Cat's realizations at the end of the book about how mean and unloving she had been to herself were mine, too—further proof that writing to yourself, even if it's disguised as fiction, really works.

So I speak from hard-won experience: Be happy with your body now, no exceptions.

We are all, all of us, the whole package: mind, body, and soul.

And in the same way we can't improve our intelligence by constantly telling ourselves how stupid we are, we can't help our bodies find their best health and appearance if we're always doing battle with them, making sure they know how dissatisfied and angry we are with how they look.

Today let's begin a new, loving relationship with the physical part of ourselves.

Perfection is a myth. And it's a damaging one that keeps us from fully enjoying our lives right now. It's time to fix that.

We can want something different for ourselves without hating and condemning where we are. That kind of disappointment in ourselves is a poison that keeps us tired and weak and ineffective in boldly moving forward so that we can claim the best for ourselves in every area of our lives.

So how do we begin to change this? By committing to loving—not just accepting, but *loving*—our wonderful bodies exactly as they are. We can want the best for them in the future and still love them now in their current wonderful form.

I'll confess that I'm still always interested in food: what I should eat, what I'm going to eat, what I just ate, what other people are eating—it's a slight obsession, but one that I actually enjoy. What's changed is that I no longer use it as a weapon against myself: *You just ate two bowls of ice cream! How could you? For the next two days it's nothing but broccoli and rice for you!*

Now the conversation might start the same, but it ends very differently: *You just ate two bowls of ice cream! I bet you loved that! Wait until you're hungry again, and see what you want then.*

And more often than not, what I want is a piece of fruit or some grilled zucchini, or maybe nothing. Because two bowls of ice cream might feel like the perfect dinner. And now that I'm not punishing myself for that, I don't have to add in a big salad on top of it just to feel like I've been "good."

The thing about any kind of obsession over how you look or what you weigh or what you eat is that it ends up *wasting so much of your time*. In retrospect, I realize I could have used all those countless hours and that single-minded focus to learn four more languages, write a dozen plays, take classes in auto repair, learn to fly a plane…

And the more important truth is that all of us are meant to be our own first friends. We have been with ourselves from the start, and it's right that we should be the ones to love and comfort and treat ourselves better than anyone else in the world. You've heard about the bond between twins? Your bond with yourself should be even tighter.

One test that seems helpful is asking yourself whether you would treat your dearest friend the way you treat your own body. Would you scold her? Punish her? Starve her? Tell her you wish she were prettier? Tell her she's ugly?

We owe it to ourselves to be kinder than ever when we're not feeling our absolute best—and feeling like we're pudgy or squishy or lethargic qualifies as not at our best.

Imagine putting an arm around your own shoulder. Give yourself a hug. You're wonderful just the way you are. These aren't just words, they're the feeling you can have toward yourself from this moment forward and for the rest of your life. Don't wait another second to be as loving as you possibly can to this wonderful structure that surrounds you. Love has a remarkable way of helping us sort out the best way to live.

I realize that not everyone reading this book has had weight problems. I know that some people already love their bodies exactly as they are, and always have. To you, I say bravo! That's wonderful! I'm so happy for you! Also, do you fly your own plane?

- Today pledge to yourself that you will only eat the most delicious food, and only exactly what and how much you want. You are not a garbage disposal. You do not have to eat all of something simply because you bought it or made it. One of the most profound changes you can make is learning to throw away food you no longer want. It might not have been as tasty as you wanted, or maybe you're just full, but whatever the reason it's a demonstration of ultimate control and power to be able to let it go.

- If you think you'll feel guilty for wasting food, view it from another perspective: By retraining your mind to know you will always give it only the most delicious food and in the perfect quantities for how you feel at any given moment, you also learn how much food to buy, cook, and serve to yourself. View this as an experiment that might take a little time and might require a short period of waste. In the long term, you'll have saved yourself years of waste in the form of both money and food.

- Some teachers advise standing in front of a mirror naked and learning to love your body as it is. I'm not a fan of that. If you're not, either, I can recommend this: Start noticing all the parts of your body that you do love. Maybe it's your friendly, genuine smile. Maybe it's your hands or feet. Your hair. Your ears. Whatever those parts are, make a point of actually paying attention to them throughout the day. When you catch sight of yourself in a mirror or window, when you look down and see your hands typing on the keyboard or your strong sturdy legs carrying you across the sidewalk, take a moment to appreciate and acknowledge those parts of your form that you already approve of, and keep noticing more parts that you can add every day. Your own approval can feel like such a relief if you've been fighting yourself for too long.

10

WHAT IF YOU ALWAYS WEAR CLOTHING THAT FITS?

Does your underwear hurt? Can you breathe when you're wearing those pants? Do you have to suck in your stomach all day to feel you look acceptable in a particular dress or shirt or suit? Do your bra straps leave welts? Do your shoes give you blisters?

"No more zippers," Judith told me in triumph the last time we met for lunch. She lifted the bottom of her stylish and roomy shirt to show me. She'll wear only stretchy waistbands from now on. She still looks elegant and put together, but she can eat lunch now without causing her belly pain. She loves herself, that's clear.

Years ago I went to a public reading by a woman author whose work I adored. I especially loved any of her nonfiction where she talked about her very adventurous life. To me, she was the epitome of cool.

But I was so sad for her as I watched her reading,

because she was obviously uncomfortable in her clothes. She must have gained weight since she bought them—or maybe she bought a size she aspired to fit into and still hadn't—but whatever the reason, she spent the whole evening picking at her shirt and her jacket, trying to cover herself better, when if she'd simply worn a size or two larger she could have relaxed and just focused on her book and the audience.

Because none of us cared how much she weighed. We already knew she was hardy and sturdy, and if that meant she was fifty pounds heavier than she wanted to be, who cares? We were there for *her* and her great writing, not for her looks.

But seeing her pick at her clothes all night made her seem insecure—not at all the real-life fearless heroine we'd been expecting to meet.

What do your clothing choices say about you? That you love yourself so much you'd never wear anything that made you feel bad or pinched or uncomfortable? Or that you're willing to torture your poor body as long as someone else might think you look good?

My friend Francie keeps three different sets of clothes for the three different sizes she naturally fluctuates among during the year. In the winter she might be one size, in the summer and fall, something else. She finally decided one day that it was foolish to pretend she could always fit comfortably into the same pants. She also let go of the idea that she should try to force her body to stay at the same weight every month of the year. It simply wasn't happening.

Live in reality—your body does. Acknowledge the true size it is right now. Then let it live in clothing that never hurts it in any way. Give it soft fabrics and comfortable waistbands. Allow your body to breathe.

And if it's honestly time to buy clothing a size up or a size down, do it. You never have to wait to treat yourself well. Show your body the love you want to be shown yourself. You know you're not perfect, but you still appreciate kindness every day. So does your body. Treat it like your dearest friend.

- Today look at the clothes in your closet and drawers and identify which ones actually fit you and feel good *now*. Maybe you have a whole other wardrobe of clothing you hope to fit in one day, but that isn't today. Live in reality. Be honest and give yourself a break.

- Weed out all of the aspirational clothes and put them in boxes for a later time. You don't have to dispose of them, just remove them from the lineup so you have more room to see everything that fits. You want the feeling when you open your drawers or closet that every single item of clothing is eligible for wearing right now, and will feel comfortable the moment you put it on.

- If you honestly need clothes in a size you don't currently own, you don't need to spend a fortune to take care of yourself. Go to a discount clothing store or thrift shop and try on clothing without worrying about the size on the tag. Sizes can vary wildly depending on the manufacturer, and all that really matters is how an item of clothing feels on *you*. Settle in to the process. Give yourself all the time you need to select at least a week's worth of wardrobe choices. Stop waiting. Take care of yourself today.

11

WHAT IF YOU'RE NOT IN TROUBLE?

It can be startling sometimes to realize we're still operating our lives through programming that goes as far back as our childhoods. One of the ways it reveals itself is through the things we habitually hear ourselves say.

My friend Diana had the horrible habit of always saying degrading things about herself. "It's because I'm so lazy … I'm such an idiot sometimes … Of course I would screw that up…"

Finally one day I'd had enough. "Stop saying such mean things about my friend!" Diana seemed surprised. She didn't realize what she had been doing.

"I guess I assume if I say it first," she told me, "no one else will think they need to criticize me." She had grown up in a family with a mother and older sisters who were always picking at everything Diana did. She had developed the habit of berating herself—sometimes with humor, but more often not—as a way of protecting her feelings. It must have made sense when she was younger, but now that she's a grown woman and free of her critical family, she can finally let that habit go.

Diana and I agreed on a program of mutual restoration. For the next year or so, any time we talked, we made sure we reminded each other of the truth.

"Ugh," Diana might say, "I ate a whole batch of chocolate chip cookies this weekend."

"And you're not in trouble for that," I'd tell her.

Or I might confess, "I watched eight hours *Lord of the Rings* again yesterday. I never wrote a word of my new book."

"That's okay," Diana would answer. "You're not in trouble for that."

It doesn't mean that our actions have no consequences. If you oversleep or forget to pay your bills or yell at your partner, you might have to face some reckoning as a result. But it means you've decided not to punish yourself on top of it. You're not in trouble with yourself.

Although Diana's and my program of repeating the phrase to each other helped it sink in the more and more we said it, you don't need someone on the outside telling you that you're fine. You can do that yourself.

Our ears are always the first to hear what our mouths say. Hearing something in our own voices gives the words even more power. That's why it's so important that when we speak of ourselves we use only the most supportive, loving language.

Instead of joking, "I'm sure you could see my butt from a mile away!" as a way of deflecting anyone else's comments about your weight (or in the secret hope that their response will be, "Are you kidding? You look great!"), practice either saying only positive things about yourself, or if you can't say something nice, say nothing at all.

Begin to notice how the confident people around you speak about themselves. Do you ever hear them say things like, "I'm such a dummy" or "I look like a blimp in this"? Doubtful. Truly confident people seem to understand the middle ground between bragging, which is always obnoxious and betrays a person's insecurities in a different way, and going too far in the other direction by constantly talking about all their faults, whether real or imagined.

It helps to replace old messages with new ones until the habit of speaking only well of yourself takes hold. From now on, let your ears hear words like these in your own voice, even if you just whisper them to yourself in private:

"Good for you, you did that really well."

"I'm so happy with how you just handled that."

"Thanks for wearing comfortable clothes today. I feel so much better."

Or whatever words you most need to hear throughout the day.

And try reminding yourself often, whenever you make a mistake or do something that in the past would have prompted you criticize yourself before anyone else could do it, that you're not in trouble for that. Not anymore.

You broke a glass? You're not in trouble for that. Clean

it up and move on. You gained five pounds? You're not in trouble for that. It might start to sound repetitive, and that's the point right now. You're reprogramming yourself.

As for Diana, she's completely cured herself of the habit. Last time we talked, she told me about a nightmare situation at her work, but she never once said anything negative about herself. In the past, she would have dotted a story like that with, "I'm so stupid…" or something equally mean, but this time she never said it. The problem at work was certainly negative, but Diana knew she was handling as best as she could.

She's not in trouble anymore. You're not, either.

- Today practice letting yourself off the hook. If you make a mistake, fix it, and move on. Practice telling yourself any time you need to, "You're not in trouble for that."

- Start noticing how you speak about yourself. Do you always speak kindly, or do say things you wouldn't want anyone else to say about your best friend? Stop the cruel words before they can make it all the way into your ears. Speaking well of yourself is a habit that can be learned. Start learning through daily practice.

12

WHAT IF YOU ARE THE SPECIAL OCCASION?

When was the last time you took a thorough look around at all of your possessions? Not just the ones that are visible in any given room, but also the ones that you have packed away and out of sight? If you reviewed all your possessions today, what would your overall impression be? That the owner of those items enjoys and appreciates them? That the owner loves and appreciates him- or herself? What is the condition of the items? Are they gently used? Tattered and worn out? Or do they still look brand new because they are?

After my friend Barbara's mother died, I helped her clean out her mother's house. In addition to all the obviously used clothing hanging in her closet, we found at least ten fancy, sparkly tops and five pairs of black dress pants that all still had the tags on them. They had been purchased, but never worn. Why?

"My mother liked to shop," Barbara said with a shrug. "It was entertainment for her."

"But why didn't she wear any of these?" I asked.

"She must have been have been waiting for a special occasion."

I could relate to that.

After I returned from helping Barbara, I spent the next several days decluttering my own house. I emptied drawers, I purged my closet, I was in a rampage of cleaning.

And just as I'd seen at Barbara's mother's house, in addition to clearing out all the things that I didn't want and never used, I uncovered a whole category of things I *did* like, but also never used: beautiful clothes and dishes, great-smelling lotions and bath salts, special foods—all sorts of little luxuries I held on to but never enjoyed because I was still waiting for the "right" time. The special occasion. Whatever and whenever that might be.

Then I realized that *I* was the special occasion. Already, just me, right then and there. I was living a life every single day and had been for years: doing my best, dealing with whatever came at me every day, making plans for the future and always moving forward—what about that wasn't enough? Why wasn't it special? What else was I waiting for?

Nothing! I didn't have to wait for anything. I already was special enough for my things. I could start using them right away. So I did, starting with a fancy tea I'd brought back from a trip and then left sitting in a cupboard. And it was *delicious.*

Since then, I make a point of using everything up. All my lotions, all my bubble baths—I get to smell great all the time, even if I'm the only one who might notice. I use my nice dishes—why shouldn't I get to eat on them? If I scratch them or they break, who cares? I own them and I should use them. I don't have to preserve them to impress somebody else who might come over. I can impress myself. *"Wow! Thanks for putting that toast on such a pretty plate! Just for me? How nice!"*

Are there things you're still holding on to, but saving for someone else to enjoy? Are there nice clothes in your closet or your drawers that you love wearing but never do because the occasion never seems to arrive? Today is that occasion! You are the reason. You get to use what you own, enjoy what you have. Right now, today, no more waiting for anyone else.

So please use your pretty dishes. Your special coffee mug. Wear your fancy top. Delight in your best lotion. Wear your nicest shoes. Eat that treat you've been keeping yourself from enjoying for far too long—today is the day! Move all your nice things to the front where you can see them, and then make a point of using them every chance you get.

- Is there some piece of clothing or household item that you've been storing for years, waiting the right time to use it? Do you still like it? If so, pull it out use it! If you don't like it or want it anymore, pass it along to someone else who will appreciate it and put it to use.

- Are there special meals that you cook or order as takeout only for special occasions? Do you wish you could taste that food more often? You don't have to wait. If you need frosted sugar cookies in July and not just in December, declare your own special occasion and have them. You are allowed to enjoy your life.

13

WHAT IF YOU GET TO FLOURISH?

What if you don't have special things that you've hidden away and rarely used? What if instead you've consistently deprived yourself of some of the simple pleasures you'd love?

When I wrote my novel *Love Proof*, I had the heroine, a down-on-her-luck lawyer named Sarah Henley, create what she called a Flourish List. Sarah began keeping the list during her years of poverty and deprivation. The name comes from both definitions of *flourish*: "an extraneous florid embellishment" (or as Sarah puts it, "Something I want, but don't actually need"), and "a period of thriving."

I don't know about you, but at times in my own life I have been *much* too stingy with myself. I called it frugality, but the truth was, I was sometimes too harsh with myself for no reason.

So I started making a point of purposely *not* being

frugal in various small ways. For example, whenever I got down to the last half-squeeze on my toothpaste tube, even though I could have forced out one last little bit, I decided to make a grand gesture of actually throwing it away—that's right, without it being fully empty—and went ahead and started a new tube. I've trained myself to do the same thing with bars of soap that have already broken into multiple parts that I have to gather together in a little pile in my palm just to work up a decent sud. Out they go. I'm allowed a fresh bar.

Small gestures, but psychologically important on my road out of poverty mentality.

So what changed things for me? Why did I start looking for ways to treat myself to small luxuries like that?

It began several years ago while I was backpacking in Colorado. I had an afternoon to myself when I sat out in a meadow, my faithful backpacking dog at my side, while my husband took off to fish. And as the dog and I sat there looking at the small white butterflies flitting over the meadow flowers, the thought occurred to me that those butterflies were not strictly necessary. Not in their dainty, pretty form. They could have been ugly and still done the job. Or they could have left their work to the yellow and brown butterflies—why do we need the extra? But having pretty white butterflies is a form of nature's flourish.

And that led to the companion idea that if flourish is allowed in nature, wouldn't it be all right to have some of it in my own life?

So right then and there I pulled out pen and paper and

started making my Flourish List. I spent an hour writing down all the things I'd wanted for years and years, but never allowed myself to have. I'm not talking about extravagances like a private jet or a personal chef, I'm talking about small pleasures like new, pretty sheets (even though the current ones were still in perfectly good shape); new long underwear that fit better; a new bra; high-quality lotion from one of the bath and body shops; fancy bubble bath. The most expensive item on my list was a pillow-top mattress to replace the plain old Costco mattress we'd been sleeping on for the past twenty years.

I gave myself the chance to write down everything, large or small, just to see it all on paper. And you know what? It wasn't that much. I had maybe fifteen items. Then, still sitting out in that meadow, I did a tally of what I thought it would all cost. I knew the mattress would probably be very expensive, so I estimated high (no internet connection out there in the wilderness, otherwise I could have researched actual numbers). I think I ended up estimating about $3,000 for the whole list. And that sounded pretty expensive to me. So I just put the list away and promised myself I'd start buying some of the cheaper items when we got home.

And I did. New underwear. Vanilla lotions and bubble baths. New sheets. And finally, a few months later, a pillow-top mattress, on sale, for less than $400. By the time I checked off the last item on my list, I had spent less than $1,000. That might still sound like a lot, but in the greater scheme I felt like it was too small an amount to have denied myself all those little pleasures all those many years. Especially if I had bought myself one of those items every year—other than the mattress—I know I never would have noticed the cost.

Now it's your turn. Create your own Flourish List, just like Sarah Henley and I did, and give yourself the pleasure of writing down every small or large thing you want for yourself right now. All the little treats. Maybe they're not so little—maybe this is the year you need a new car or some other big-ticket item. But that's a "Need" list. This is your Flourish List—everything you want but don't necessarily need.

Next, treat yourself. Choose one item every week or every month, and give it to yourself. And if you feel strange about replacing something you don't like with something you know you will, then remember to pass on that other item to someone else who might love it more than you did. I've done that with clothes, kitchenware, books: It feels so good to take everything you don't want and give it to a thrift store where someone else can be happy to have found it, and found it so cheaply. Maybe there's someone out there with a Flourish List that includes a pair of boots like the ones that have just been gathering dust in your closet. Stop hoarding them. Move them on to their new, appreciative owner.

And by doing that, you make room in your own life for things you'll appreciate and enjoy. It's hard to invite abundance when you're chock full of clutter. Make some room. Make your list. And then start treating yourself the way you deserve by no longer withholding those little items that you know will make you smile.

It's time for you to flourish.

- Today create your own Flourish List. Give yourself plenty of time to imagine and write, then imagine and write some more. Don't worry about whether you can afford everything that's on your list, just take the time to listen to what you want and then write everything down.

- Treat yourself. Choose one item every week or every month, and give it to yourself. It might be something as inexpensive as a new pair of fuzzy socks or a keychain that feels better in your pocket. Give yourself this love.

14

WHAT IF YOU TAKE SECRET DELIGHT IN YOUR MANY TALENTS?

Think of all the things you do in a day—things that maybe no one else appreciates. You always make your bed. You're the expert at taking care of your pets. You're a careful driver. You greet people with a genuine smile. You listen. You're a great friend. You always put out a fresh roll of toilet paper when you notice the other one is about to run out.

I'm serious: You get credit for these things. Credit with yourself, at least. But only if you actually make a point of noticing.

Secret delight and secret pride can take the place of waiting for other people to thank you for what you've done or to show you that they value some aspect of your personality. Of course it would be thrilling to go through a day getting regular recognition—"Look at you, refilling the water in the coffee pot when no one else thought to do it!

And the way you handled that phone call just now! Wow, well done!"—but that's probably not going to happen. But how much nicer would a day be if you took the few extra moments throughout it to give yourself your own little bit of applause?

Resist the temptation to point out your accomplishments and good deeds to any of the people around you. It can make you seem needy and insecure, and if the people don't react the way you want them to you will be disappointed. It's better to treasure your triumphs in your heart and feel good about what you can do. It's part of building your own internal success file. Every new thing you notice is yet another item on the list.

There is a teaching in martial arts that the higher the rank you achieve, the more humble you should be. It's the lower ranking fighters who feel the need to swagger as they walk down the middle of a road. The highest ranked master walks to the side of the road, content not to draw attention to himself. He knows who he is and what he's capable of, and is supremely confident in his skills. He doesn't need to blare his accomplishments to the world. In other words, be cool.

I think of my *Sensei* Gregg, a seventh degree black belt. He has the ability to enter a room at work so silently and drawing so little attention to himself, his coworkers often don't know he's there until he speaks. Although he might not admit it, he must take secret pride in that.

My friend Francie is in charge of all of her family finances—not because she wants to be, but because her husband has no interest in it. They're both lawyers, both capable of doing the same careful work, but for the entire thirty years they've been together, she alone has paid all the bills, kept up with the bookkeeping, and dealt with their tax returns. It's a lot of work on top of her regular job, and she wishes she didn't have to do it alone.

"But can't you take secret delight in being so good at it?" I've asked her.

"No! You and your secret delight!"

I'll keep working to convince her. In the meantime I can take secret pride in knowing I'm right.

- Today notice all the things you do so well. Notice your diligence and competence from the time you wake up until you fall asleep. You know how people just beginning to fall in love seem to notice every little thing about their partner? Give yourself *that* level of attention and appreciation. Really bask in your own admiration.

- The next time you feel tempted to point out something nice you've just done for someone or to remind that person to tell you thank you—don't. Instead, take secret pride in your ability to do great things for other people without requiring any recognition in return. Take secret pride in the fact that you're cool.

15

WHAT IF YOU TEACH PEOPLE HOW TO TREAT YOU?

How we present ourselves in the world can send a signal to others about how they should treat us and behave around us. You have more power than you know.

Janet, one of the *Senseis* or master instructors at my dojo, is warm, loving, funny, and clearly not to be messed with. Now in her 60s, she can still punch, kick, and throw much younger opponents, but you wouldn't have to watch her doing that to know she's tough.

She and I have taught numerous girls' and women's self-defense classes together, and I've gotten used to the initial reaction of some of our students: "She scares me!" To which I always answer with a smile, "That's right."

One of the things we teach the women in our classes is how to stand tall and carry themselves confidently, already signaling to the world even at a distance that they are alert, strong (no matter how physically strong they may or may not actually be), and that they can handle themselves in dicey situations. Our goal, we tell the students, is never to have to fight. So in addition to teaching good safety practices and situational awareness, we also teach the girls and women how to present themselves in such a way that if an aggressor were scanning a crowd looking for a likely target, our students would seem like the least attractive victims. They look like they would be trouble. That's right.

One of the things I've learned from observing Janet over the years is that she never talks down about herself. She isn't a braggart—far from it—but you would never hear her joking, "I'm such a klutz," or "Yep (slapping her hip), I really like to pack it in." She treats herself with dignity. If she speaks of herself at all, it's with respect. And what I've noticed is that everyone around her seems to follow her example and treat her the same way.

The few times I've seen someone cross the line and try to touch her in a way that wasn't welcome or speak to her in a way that was demeaning or otherwise unacceptable, she didn't laugh it off or try to make the other person feel comfortable with what they'd done. If the moment was awkward, which it clearly was, that was the other person's fault, not hers. It wasn't Janet's job to fix it or make them feel fine about what they'd done. Instead, she has a way of looking at any offender that leaves no room for doubt: *"If you do that again, you will regret it."*

Is that mean of her? No. Is that rude? No. We are allowed to teach people how to treat us. In fact, even without intending to, we are teaching people how to treat us all the time.

Do you go along with things that make you uncomfortable simply because you don't want to make a fuss? Is it more important for someone to like you and think you're nice than to take care of yourself in the ways that you need? Are you that dependable person who will always say yes to a request, even when everything inside you wishes you would say no?

You don't have to continue that way. You can change right now, in an instant. Treating yourself with dignity and care is a skill that improves quickly the more you practice. The good news is that there are multiple opportunities every single day for not talking down about yourself; walking upright and carrying yourself with confidence; saying no if that is your honest answer; and practicing a whole host of other behaviors that can transform you in the ways that you want.

Being strong and confident isn't a matter of muscle or even toughness. It's simply showing the people around you that you respect and value yourself, and that you expect them to do the same.

- Today notice how you stand and walk. How is your posture? Do you slump forward, always reading your phone? Or do you walk tall, eyes forward and alert, stride confident and strong? Your naturally upright and relaxed posture has a double effect: It conveys confidence to the people around you, while also making you feel more confident inside your body and in your surroundings. Try it. You'll be surprised by how easily it can change the way you feel.

- If someone treats you with disrespect, practice not smiling or laughing just to smooth over the moment or make the offender feel more comfortable. That isn't your job. The person *should* feel uncomfortable. You don't have to frown or glower, simply keep your expression neutral and don't race to fill the air with words. Better yet, walk away. That person has just lost the privilege of your presence.

- It's better to avoid a fight than to have to win it. If you ever sense that a person or a situation is dangerous, trust your instinct. Go no further. Turn around and get out. Your life and your safety are precious. You don't have to prove that you're strong. Taking care of yourself by staying clear of danger is always the strongest and smartest move.

16

WHAT IF YOU ACCEPT PEOPLE'S KINDNESS?

Do you secretly think you don't deserve the good things that come your way?

It's a hard thing to admit. It's much easier to pretend that good things don't show up. But we all know they *do*. You find a dollar on the ground. Do you leave it for someone else, either because the rightful owner might come back looking for it and be upset that it's lost, or because someone coming after you might need it more? Would it make a difference if it were a dime or quarter or penny instead? Would you pick that up?

Someone offers to do you a favor, and you're not sure you have anything of value to give in return. Do you say no because you can't reciprocate?

You find out about a contest or grant or some other opportunity that sounds just perfect for you, but you hesitate to take the step of entering or applying. Why? Because you might actually get it? Or because if you get it then someone else won't?

Whatever the reason, you might have developed a habit over the years of constantly turning away from your good. But like any habit, you can change it and start gratefully accepting the things that you want.

My friend Larissa has been having a terrible time with her job. She doesn't just hate it, it's actively harming her health. She's been planning to quit for the past six months. But every time I talk to her, she's moved the date forward by another few months.

"I just need to save a little more money," she told me recently. "I'm sure I'll have it by December." (Which is what she said last time, but the month back then was August.)

And meanwhile she looks like she could go to bed for a year and still not cure all her stress and exhaustion.

This time when we talked she casually mentioned that her boyfriend for the last two years offered to support her for a few months while she looked for another job.

Hallelujah, I thought. *"And???"*

"Come on, you know I don't do that," she said. "I've never done that."

But she admitted she knows she's running herself into the ground, and that she's far from a joy to be around. By the time she gets home at night, she's got nothing left. Plus she's lost weight, she has no energy—she knows she has to get out.

"Please, let him help you," I said. "You know he means it, and he can afford it."

"But I don't do that," she still insisted.

We love our friends, but sometimes they really do need a tender knock upside the head.

So I told her what I see: That she has this habit of keeping all sorts of nice things circling above her head like planes in a holding pattern, and if she'd just let them start landing, she'd be so much happier and more relaxed. It's just these rules she's made up for herself that keep her from accepting kindnesses that people in her life have sincerely offered.

"If he didn't mean it," I argued, "he wouldn't offer. He means it. He wants to help you. He wants his happy girlfriend back. *Let him.*"

The most I could get from her was, "I'll think about it." At least that's progress.

Although Larissa's might seem like an extreme example, we've all done this in our lives. We turn away from kindnesses that other people have offered. Why? Do we think it's the polite thing to do? Do we think we'll look weak or greedy if we accept?

Or maybe we will eventually accept, but first we have to go through a certain ritual: Two or three adamant refusals while the kind person continues insisting, and then finally, reluctantly, our yes.

Can't we drop the performance? Or is it that we honestly don't believe we deserve nice things? We have to keep sitting in the mud digging for worms to eat while someone is holding out a perfectly lovely cake. Take the cake!

Maybe that's why it's so noticeable whenever I see someone immediately say yes. My friend Kirsten shows me by example that it's fine to accept the good.

She came over to my house to drop something off, and I knew she'd been running errands for hours. Polite hostess that I am, I followed the polite hostess script.

"Do you want something to eat?" I asked her. "Something to drink?"

"Yes," she said with obvious relief, "I would love that."

I was a little startled, only because people don't normally respond that way. I'm used to, "No, that's okay, I'm fine," even if the person is actually famished.

But Kirsten is brave that way. Good for her. So I made her a nice afternoon snack of toast and strawberry jam along with a fresh cup of coffee.

And do you know what? I felt *great* about that. It felt nice to take care of my friend.

That's the thing about someone offering you a kindness: It isn't only for you. People like to think of themselves as kind and generous. They like to do nice things—especially if you're a nice person yourself. They might want to give you gifts or pay for your meal or go out of their way to help you even when you know it's an inconvenience.

Let them.

And instead of arguing, offer them a happy, sincere, heart-felt, "Thank you so much! That's so wonderful of you. I really appreciate it." It's what they actually prefer to hear. You're doing them a kindness by gracefully accepting their gift. Well done. Niceness all around.

So the next time someone offers to do something generous or kind for you, try skipping the ritual of, "Oh no, I can't! It's too much! You shouldn't have!"

Yes you can, no it's not, and yes they should. Give all those kindnesses circling over your head a welcome place to land.

- Today notice how you feel when you offer a kindness to other people: Do you hope they'll turn it down, or do you really hope they accept? If they do accept, how do you feel then? Do you enjoy doing something nice for someone else? Does it make you think well of yourself?

- Consider that others feel as you do. The next time someone offers you a kindness, accept graciously and let them feel kind.

- What are the things you know you could have in your life right now, if only you'd turn toward them instead of away from them? An opportunity of some kind? An offer to help you in some way? Someone's friendship or love? What's been holding you back? What would it feel like if you said yes?

17

WHAT IF YOU'RE ALLOWED TO LEARN AS MUCH AS YOU WANT TO?

Part of living your unique life is finding out everything you want to know about anything. Diving in deep to the things you're passionate about is never a waste of time.

One of my absolute favorite things about starting any new book project is thinking about all the research I'll get to do. I never have to justify to anyone why I need to read a stack of books about medieval history or quantum physics or reincarnation. I love to know a whole lot of different things, and what those things are is very specific to me. I use the information to write stories that I hope will entertain my readers, too, but my honest motivation is always my own desire to learn more all the time.

What kinds of information do you love to know? Do you ever feel embarrassed about that? Have other people made fun of you—even in a "good natured" way (personally, I never find teasing to be good natured)—for the many obscure details you know about something other people have decided is boring?

Who cares what they think?

Learning what we're interested in knowing is never boring—to us. It's never frivolous. Because learning what we in particular are interested in knowing is part of our own particular lives. It's part of our own unique path. It's never for someone else to judge whether we *need* to know what we're interested in knowing —that's our own business entirely. Just as how much sleep and what kind of food our own particular bodies needs is specific to us.

Hermione Granger in the *Harry Potter* series is such a great model for the person who happily pursues knowledge for the sake of knowing everything. And boy, does it pay off. But she wasn't learning everything she could about magic and the history of Hogwarts because she wanted to save her friends one day, she learned because she was interested. Fascinated, in fact. And that led to all kinds of great consequences later, just as you learning all the things you're interested in will bring you great wonders in your own life.

How do I know? Because I read a lot of biographies of people in the arts and adventure worlds. And what I've seen over and over is that people who became great leaders and innovators—and great survivors, in the case of disasters of various sorts—are the ones who accumulated vast amounts of knowledge in the areas that captured their interest, and they then got to use that knowledge in surprising and yet completely perfect (in hindsight) ways.

Take Steve Jobs of Apple computers fame. He dropped out of college and then took a few classes here and there in subjects that interested him. One of those was calligraphy, which later led to him developing a personal computer with various font choices.

Another is Walt Disney, pushing his animators not only to learn how to do animation better, but how to do *art* better. He hired an art instructor to teach them about anatomy, about skeleton and musculature and movement, and it was that extra knowledge that helped the Disney animation move so far ahead of anything that had been done before.

If you looked at your own life, and looked at it as a *story*, you could identify things you've done or learned or experienced that might have made no practical sense at the time, but later turned out to be absolutely crucial to what you needed at a particular moment.

All of this is a way of saying that if you're interested in something, that's the only justification you need for pursuing it—and for pursuing it hard. If you want to read everything you can get your hands on about a particular topic, do it. Even if you're not sure it will ever "pay off" in some tangible way.

Because the "payoff" is *you*. You're allowed to be excited about knowing the things you're excited about knowing. You're here to live your own life, and that includes pursuing the knowledge that appeals to you. Living a full life is always the justification for chasing after your own dreams and passions. You never have to explain yourself beyond that.

- Are there classes you're interested in taking to learn more about a particular skill? What's holding you back? Dive in! Your own interest in it is justification enough. It's a simple way of enjoying your own life, and that's justification enough, too.

18

WHAT IF YOU CAN DO AS MANY OCCUPATIONS AS YOU WANT?

Are you stuck believing that you have to pick one thing to pursue as a career, and so you'd better get it right? What if you can do multiple things at once? Or multiple different things one after another throughout your whole interesting life?

One of the people my friend Christine met in her new mountain town was a woman named Sarah who both taught science at the local school and started her own nonprofit composting business.

There were plenty of environmentally conscious people in that rural area who would have loved to compost their food scraps in compost heaps of their own, but no one could do it in their own gardens or yards because the food would attract bears.

Sarah realized there was a need, and she decided to do something about it. It was obviously one of her Uses. She applied for grants and held fundraisers and also charged her customers a small monthly fee for coming to their houses in her pickup truck and dumping their buckets of compost into larger containers of her own. Then she brought all the material back to an enclosed area that she rented and allowed decomposition to do its thing.

Not only were her customers happy that they no longer had to just throw into the garbage all their banana peels and strawberry husks and eggs shells, but those customers could also get back from Sarah buckets full of beautiful, rich, compost-created dirt that they could mix into their own soil to feed their trees and other plants.

Win-win-win.

What if Sarah had the attitude that she was a teacher, and that was it? Or if my lawyer friend Christine thought she could only be a lawyer? She had paid for that expensive degree, after all, and she had put in all that time and effort (a point her family and friends were always eager to remind her of), and she had just "thrown it all away" to go live in the country and be a writer and take painting classes and make and can her own jam.

Sounds pretty heavenly to me.

You have multiple skills and interests, too. How do I know? We all do. It's just that we sometimes get into a mindset of believing we should only do one career in our adult lives or only one career at a time.

But what if you have the skills and the desire to be a musician *and* a business owner *and* a dog breeder *and* an ultra-marathoner? Is there some law that says you can't apportion your time accordingly and do all of those things in the same year?

Perhaps in generations past it was practical to choose only one career or job and stick with it. But these are modern times, and new opportunities arise every day not only to create a business, job, or career that uses some or all of your skills, but also to reach out to people all over the world who might share your interests and need exactly what you have to offer.

You have many Uses. You're allowed to express as many of those as you choose, whether one at a time, one after another, or a whole bucket of them all at once.

- Today ask yourself whether there's more that you'd like to do. It might be more in your current situation, such as adding a side business that incorporates one of your hobbies or another one of your Uses, or it might mean stopping what you're doing entirely and moving on to a new job or career.

- If it's a side business or project, what steps can you begin today to organize your existing blocks of time and make room for something new? Are there things you'll be happy to get rid of? Do you need to limit some of the others? A helpful tool is to imagine what you would do if you were suddenly faced with a crisis and had to rearrange your obligations to deal with it. What changes would you make to the current demands on your time? Now, go ahead and skip the crisis and just go straight for the change. Free up your time for yourself so you can do all that you'd love to do.

- Do you feel like you've gotten all that you can out of your current occupation, and you're ready to move on? If you feel guilty for wanting to leave your current occupation, consider that people got good value from you while you were there. They had a good run. You gave the job or career what you had to offer, and now you're going to apply your value to something else. We can be happy for what we've contributed to a place without feeling obligated to stay there forever.

- Look around you for examples and inspiration. Is there someone you admire who is on their fourth or fifth career? When I went to law school, there were plenty of older students who wanted to become lawyers after years spent as something else. I met doctors, business people, a nail technician, even a former county coroner. Those people gave good value in their former work, and they were ready to give good value again.

19

WHAT IF YOU PUT YOURSELF FIRST?

What if putting yourself first isn't selfish, but is a wise and practical thing to do?

Every few years I spend several days going through training to be recertified as a wilderness medic (specifically a Wilderness First Responder). And every time, the people I meet in the course are just as fascinating as the lessons themselves.

It's probably no surprise that I'm always the only writer in the group. Everyone else works as a wilderness or river guide, park ranger, search and rescue leader, recovery diver—the list varies. In my most recent class there were also a few field scientists in the group who spend months at a time in third-world countries where there isn't a lot of medical help nearby. You'd be amazed at some of the emergencies a traveling geologist has to deal with.

My most important takeaway from that recent recertification wasn't about new medical techniques, it was about the first rule that has always been drilled into our heads.

A little background: Whenever we come upon a scene where there's someone injured, we've been taught to go through a checklist:

Number 1: I'm number one. So look around, check the area, make sure it's safe for me, the rescuer.

Number 2: What happened to you? Look at the injured person from a distance and make an initial evaluation: How hurt does he or she look? Is he dead or alive?

And so on, down a list of numbers.

We're constantly drilled on the issue of scene safety, making sure that we protect ourselves with gloves and other safety equipment, but this time I got a new perspective on that rule.

It came from two separate conversations I had with two of the most experienced people in the group: the instructor and one of the participants, both of them ex-soldiers with a long list of post-military jobs in various rescue professions.

They shared with me their own journeys as rescuers: First, thinking that they needed to save everyone they came across; later feeling dejected when they couldn't save everybody after all; then learning the sobering truth by watching colleagues get injured or die from helping others that yes, they as rescuers really ARE number one, and their first responsibility is to protect themselves. It does no one any good for either of them to be hurt or killed trying to save someone else. They knew that in theory, but they've seen it in practice too many times to ignore it.

Good Samaritans drown, one of them told me. They get electrocuted. Overcome by smoke. He told me stories about all of those. He said he never stops to help when he sees an accident on the highway because it's too dangerous. Too many rescuers get hit by cars themselves. He said he always pulls off as soon as he can and calls 911. Then he lets the emergency personnel on duty that day take care of the injured people.

He pointed out that even when the paramedics arrive, they don't just race in to help, they wait until highway patrol has set up road blocks to make the accident scene safe. There's a specific protocol to follow, and professionals take it seriously. Their lives depend on it.

The other guy said that he had to train himself to be detached and to do only his own work during his own shift and stop looking around for all the people who might need saving.

"I had to tell myself, 'That's not my emergency.'" he said. "There are other people doing the same thing I am, with the same skills, and it's their turn. I have to take care of myself. I have to get enough sleep. I have to be fit and healthy. There will always be people who need help. I can't be on 24/7."

He said his mantra of "That's not my emergency" also helps him remember that he can only do what he can—he didn't create this person's situation. So if he can't get to the patient quickly enough or can't save him once he does ... then that's what happened. It was that patient's emergency, not his. He did the best that he could.

How does this apply to civilians like you and me? The situations we face might not be life-or-death every day, but it's still worth remembering Rule #1: "I'm number one." You owe it to yourself to make decisions that protect you first. That protect your peace of mind, your financial stability, your safety, your health, your happiness. YOU MATTER. Your life matters.

Still, is it hard for you to imagine doing this? Does it sound selfish? Unfriendly? Mean? Are you so used to putting everyone else's needs before your own, you're not even sure you'd know how to do things differently?

One revealing question Janet and I ask the students in our self-defense classes is whether they feel comfortable really hurting their attacker. How hard would they be willing to fight to protect and save their own lives? Some of the answers are lukewarm: "Not sure I could do that. Gouge somebody in the eye? Take out his knee? No way."

Then we ask how hard they would fight if it were to protect their child or their partner or their friend or even their pet. *Then* the answers are different. Suddenly everyone is a ferocious mother bear.

To which we always ask: *Why would you do that for someone else, but not for yourself?*

The truth is you are better able to help others when you are safe and well yourself. So if you need to rest, go ahead and rest. If you need to say no this time, say no. Continue to give yourself adequate time every day to make your life as healthy and fulfilling as you want. Once you've taken care of yourself, you can choose how much time and energy you want to share with other people. Think of the rescue professionals: They enjoy living their own lives in between their shifts.

And if the people in your life are constantly coming to you to solve their various crises, maybe it's worth reminding yourself, "That's not my emergency." You didn't create it, and you're not required to solve it. Fair means fair to you too, and that means you get to enjoy your own life as much as you can.

It's just like the flight attendants always tell us: Put on your own oxygen mask first.

- Today be conscious of the times when you rush right in to fix something—specifically some problem or crisis that you didn't create yourself. How did you feel when you did that? Were you proud to be able to help, or did your efforts feel like a burden? Next time consider holding yourself back and see how that feels, too. Do you miss being part of the solution? Or are you happy to be free of the trouble?

20

WHAT IF SAYING NO CAN FEEL AS COMFORTABLE AS SAYING YES?

Do you have a hard time telling people you like, "No"? What if sometimes "no" is the nicer answer?

Recently the call went out from one of my beloved cousins that it's time for another cousin reunion, this time in a beautiful seaside town where we can all share a house together for a week.

Yes! Absolutely! To the reunion. No, no way to the house part.

Why? Because some people are tribal, and some are not. I love my family and love spending lots of time with them, but I also need to be able to get away. To go somewhere quiet for a while so I can rest and recharge, instead of getting to the point where I'm so overstimulated I end up not being any fun.

I used to make the mistake of going along with things to "be a good sport," but it always backfired. Because I don't know about you, but whenever I do something to be a good sport, I end up feeling like people should appreciate the effort I'm making. It's completely petty and unfair, but I'm just going to tell the truth: I want people to think, *"Wow, look how she's putting herself out here. We know she hates this kind of thing. She must be a really good person for going along."*

What a ridiculous burden to put on anyone else. Plus, no one ever actually thinks that. Because isn't it more reasonable to assume that if someone has shown up to an event—a party or an outing or a trip—he or she actually wants to be there? Seems rational. Anything else seems a little crazy.

So rather than show up places and be all poopy-pants about it (*"I'm here! This better be fun! I could have been home reading a book!"*), I've just gotten used to being honest and saying no when I'm not excited about whatever's being offered. That way my yes, when it comes, is a real honest-to-goodness yes. And I can go into it knowing that it's what I actually *want*.

Think about the things you go along with in your own life. Are you truly a volunteer? Do you say yes only when you really mean yes? Or are you still hoping you get all sorts of credit for being a good sport, even if you're actually a *bad* good sport?

One thing that helped me understand that it's actually okay to say no and that people wouldn't be mad is that I started paying attention to how I felt when someone else told me no. Yes, I prefer to get my way all the time—don't we all?—but whenever someone told me straight out, "No, but thanks for asking, " or "No, I won't be able to do that," I was fine. Perfectly fine. I didn't hold a grudge, I wasn't angry, we all went on with our lives.

So if you're still caught up in saying yes far more times than you mean it, I invite you to start noticing that same thing: Isn't "no" an okay thing to hear? Do you maybe even admire the people who can confidently say no to something without falling all over themselves apologizing?

In fact, have you noticed that some people have developed a reputation for always saying no, and so people tend to leave them alone? "Don't ask Rachel to a party. She never comes." By training the people around her for a while, Rachel has saved herself from continuing to have to refuse invitations.

Think of people you know who have made deliberate changes in their lives. Maybe someone has become vegetarian or stopped drinking. Friends might still try to offer them meat or beer for a period of time, but eventually everyone understands the new policy.

We are constantly showing people how to treat us. If you want to switch from being the go-to reliable person who will always agree to everything, to now being the person who hardly says yes at all—then go for it. People adjust when they have to. You're allowed to refuse the things you don't want.

So here's to the no. The good no. The no that says, "Nah, that's not really for me, but thanks for thinking of me anyway!"

And here's to our real yesses that really come from the heart.

- Today think before you agree to something. Decide whether you really, truly want to say yes or no. Also consider whether you're expecting credit for going along with something you don't really enjoy.

- Skip the credit. People don't usually give it out anyway. Instead give yourself credit every single time today when you say yes *only* if you mean it.

21

WHAT IF FAILURE IS ONLY A TEMPORARY CONDITION?

There is a difference between failing at something and feeling like a failure. We all fail at times, and it's something we should all be able to admit. But feeling like a failure is a step too far, and is worth resisting whenever we can.

How we feel about failure seems directly tied to our expectations. If we assume we will do a particular thing well, we feel stung and embarrassed when we fall short. But if we're about to do something we've never tried before or that we already know is not our best skill, we seem much better able to give ourselves a break.

Why can't we apply that same level of forgiveness to all of our mistakes? The answer is that we can, of course. We just have to become more aware of the ways in which we are less than kind to ourselves on those occasions when we mess up.

We all take pride in ourselves for certain things. I like to think of myself as a diligent, competent person. And so any time I slip up on something I normally assume I will be perfect at—paying a bill on time, cooking a meal I've cooked fifty times before, remembering someone's birthday—that really does feel like a failure to me, and it would be all too easy to be ruthlessly critical of myself.

On the other hand, if someone invited me to come play golf—something I've never done before and have zero expectation of being even mildly good at—I would have a good attitude and be able to laugh at every bad swing and wild response of the ball. Failing at golf would not lower my opinion of myself in any way.

If you reflect back over your own past few days, you can probably identify the minor failures that you cared about too much and that caused you at least some degree of distress, and then the other ones that you were able to shrug off quickly because they truly meant nothing to your life. Were your expectations of your own competence different on those occasions? Can you imagine treating yourself kindly the next time you fail in some way, whether or not you expected yourself to succeed?

And so what if you do just outright fail some of the time? Is that the end of the story?

I read a lot of biographies, and it's always surprising to learn how many times my heroes of history failed. Failed *big*. And not just in one period of their lives and then everything else was glorious, but failed this year and that year and for all of these years in a row.

Their failure was not their story. Their story was in trying again. The reason we care about these great people at all is that they failed a lot and kept going.

You have a story, too. And it's longer and more exciting that whatever mistake you just made. Your failures might be an interesting anecdote one day, a side story you might choose to tell. But the principal story, the one we all want to see, is how you shook it all off and kept on.

- Today when you make any kind of mistake (the odds are good that we all will), notice how much you do or don't care. Are there some mistakes that you shrug and shake your head about, and others that make you feel awful for hours? What made the difference? Was it a matter of your expectations, whether other people witnessed it, or some other factor?

- Also observe other people around you when they make mistakes (again, the odds are good). How do they react to their failures? Do they become defensive? Embarrassed? Or do some seem to take it all in stride? Are you ready to start taking yours in stride, too?

22

WHAT IF YOU SIMPLY APOLOGIZE TO YOURSELF AND MOVE ON?

How much time do you spend every day replaying any of the vast multitude of mistakes you've made during your life? They might be mistakes from ten years ago or five minutes ago: Our minds seem to have an endless capacity for going over and over our flubs, our moral failings, all of the things we said and wished we hadn't, the things we wished we'd done or not done.

Most of that is a complete waste of time.

Regret does serve a purpose: It shows us what we wish we had done better. That's it. That's its job. And it is to our advantage to take that information and use it to do better next time. Because until physicists have perfected time travel for the average person, science simply will not allow us to go back and relive the moments we regret and do them any differently. So we have to come up with a more workable plan. Here it is:

Apologize to yourself and move on.

Apologize to *yourself*? That's right. But what about all the other people you might have hurt or could have treated better?

Accept that you were not the good person you wish you had been—which is actually a hard thing to admit to ourselves sometimes—and apologize to your current self for once again failing to get it right. It feels bad to know we're not always as great as we mean to be. It hurts to see ourselves fail.

You can also apologize to other people if you feel that is the appropriate step to take, but it isn't necessary for purposes of this remedy. The issue here is how all of us waste so much time by allowing our minds to be caught in an endless whirlpool of regret, going over and over something that has already happened and is past. It's over. Move on. Go forth and be much, much better.

Here is a minor example: I have apologized to myself for all the decades when I made myself go on diets, beginning when I was in sixth grade. What was I thinking? Why was I so mean to myself? It created a cycle of obsession, disappointment, and punishment that was very damaging to my spirit and never actually brought me the lasting change I wanted. And now that I've finally relaxed about all of it, I am a size that is completely comfortable for me. I can do all the sports I want, I feel healthy and alert, and though I wear clothes a few sizes larger than I did when I was younger, who cares? Honestly, NO ONE CARES.

But for a while I was really punishing myself mentally

about having wasted so much of my own time and good will by not being happy inside my own body.

Notice that I didn't regret having ever *been* a bigger size or heavier than I wanted—I had already finally gotten past that particular meanness—but here I was turning my fresh indignant criticism toward the younger version of myself who had been so bossy and insecure that she needed to make my weight such a big issue for me in the first place.

Total waste of time. Hours spent scolding myself: *How could you be so mean? Howww??? Do you understand what you did??? You really hurt my feelings!* Please. I could have put that time and emotional energy to so much better use.

That's when I realized the only possible cure was to apologize to myself and move on. *Sorry I tried to make you feel bad about making me feel bad. Friends now? Great. Let's go do something fun.* It worked miraculously well. Try it.

And after you've made your apology, store away the information offered to you by your regret and promise you'll do things differently next time. Don't only promise, do that. It's a mark of intelligence and our own personal advancement in life to be able to make smarter choices based on what we've learned from the really bad ones.

Next time you catch yourself wasting time regretting your all-too-human capacity for doing exactly what you wish you hadn't done, apologize to yourself for not being great. It happens more often than we can think we can bear. But all we can do, any of us, is step right back on our superior path and do our best to do better *next time*.

- Today apologize to yourself for whatever it is you regret in your past. Accept that it happened. It wasn't good. Maybe *you* weren't as good as you wish you had been. Today is a fresh day. Be who you want to be. Imagine dropping this burden at the side of the road and finally walking away free.

- And today, do better. Live up to your current standards. That's the best repayment you can make for any debt you feel you owe.

- Use the power of "next time." Get used to telling yourself that as often as you need. Skip the step where you curse and berate yourself—what possible purpose does that serve?—and instead speed straight to the analysis of what went wrong and what you can do right next time. Be proactive on your own behalf. Pretend you are trying to correct the trajectory of a rocket that keeps spinning out of control and crashing. You don't have time to waste regretting that the last ten tries didn't make it. Figure out what went wrong. Fix your math. Do something better next time.

23

WHAT IF MAKING CHANGES IS EASIER THAN YOU THINK?

What if you decide that the time has come in your life when you do want to make some changes? The only way to change is to change. It sounds obvious, but it really isn't.

So often when we decide to make a change of some kind, we feel like we have to take a running start, get ready, here it comes, just a few days from now, I mean it.... We have to tell everyone around us, "Okay! I'm doing it! Brace yourselves!" But maybe we have to do a few preparations first: Eat all the sugar in the house so it won't be there to tempt us, clean a few closets, go on a trip, watch three or four movies—our techniques vary depending on how big the upcoming change feels.

But what if you skipped all that drama? Can you just decide to change something, change it, and continue on?

You can.

There are two different methods: One is to decide first what you want to do, how you want to behave, how you want to look, what dreams you want to pursue—the whole big-picture plan. It's as if you're looking at the earth from space: View your whole ideal life on a grand scale first, then move your focus closer so you can examine in greater detail every aspect of what you want.

This is a perfect time for using the tools of writing to yourself and asking yourself questions. Set aside a reasonable block of time when you can be alone and unhurried, and then let your imagination feel free. If some of your ideas about how you want to be and live feel too personal for anyone else to see right now, you can always deliver your papers to the shredder when you're done. But for now write continuously and let all of your ideas pour out. Interview yourself either out loud or on paper. Give yourself the time and attention you need.

Then, when you feel satisfied that you've described yourself and your ideal life in as much detail as you can, switch to a new sheet of paper and start writing out your steps. Everything has steps. Even blinking has steps. Your eyelids begin lowering, a quarter of the way, now half … you could break down the elements of a blink into a dozen separate steps if you tried.

Make your steps distinct and achievable all by themselves. You want the pleasure of being able to check off as many as you can every week or even every day.

And finally, start doing. The only way to change is to

change, so do it. One thing at a time, spare the drama, just do it. Then keep going until you're there.

The second method approaches change from the opposite direction. Instead of using your thoughts to change your behavior, you allow your behavior to change how you are.

You might have heard of a term from the field of psychology known as "cognitive dissonance": We feel discomfort whenever we behave in ways that go against our beliefs, ideas, or values. You can use that discomfort to help yourself become how you truly want to be.

If you see yourself being kind to people, you think of yourself as a kind person. If you see yourself being outdoorsy and athletic, you think of yourself that way. You might achieve the same results by telling yourself, *"From now on, I'm going to be kind and outdoorsy and athletic!"* but for some of us it's actually easier to start the new behaviors right away and just keep doing them, rather than make any big pronouncements and then try to live up to them.

I don't need a certificate from some outside authority to tell me I'm a writer. I know that I am because I can see what I do. I write something every day, whether it's the pages of my journal or song lyrics or scenes in a novel or a short story. Some of my projects might be more successful than others, but my own perception of myself as a writer doesn't change based on the world's reaction to what I make.

If I were still a lawyer and decided I would rather be a writer, I might make a list of all things I intended to do to pursue that dream and then begin ticking them off one by one.

Or I might just write something right now. A few lines of a song. An opening paragraph of a novel. Just something to show myself in an instant that this is who I am now. *Look, I can prove it: I'm already doing it.*

If it's some quality that you would like to develop such as being calmer, you could use the first method to think ahead about situations that set you off and how you plan to deal with them differently from now on. Having thought through stressful events and your preferred response at your leisure, you're better prepared to deal with them if and when they arrive. Imagine first, then do.

Or, using the opposite approach, you can decide to wait for the next stressful event (which won't take too long, life being what it is) and change your habitual reaction on the spot so that you can enjoy watching yourself being calm. *That's how I am now.*

You know best which method appeals to your way of thinking and to your personality. If you're a list maker, you might enjoy the process of designing your life detail by specific detail. But if that process sounds time-consuming or not to your taste, consider jumping right in and doing first, then watching yourself take those actions. The more you continue behaving your way toward new habits, the more quickly those habits will feel more natural. One day you will notice you're there. You already are whatever it is. Great. Keep going.

- Today take time to write down the details of how you see yourself in your new changed way. How do you look? How do you carry yourself in the world? Are you smiling? Are you relaxed? What kind of work are you doing? Who are your friends? What kind of passion projects do you see yourself pursuing? Write it all down. Have a blast. Really give yourself the big, full picture.

- Then on a separate sheet of paper begin listing all the steps you see yourself taking to walk forward to meet that changed edition of yourself. Are there some of those steps you can take immediately? What if you don't have to wait to smile, but can do it right now? What if you can be relaxed now, not just a year from now? If you have some passion project in mind, can you start it right away? What's stopping you? Go ahead and make a move. The more you begin taking action toward your new life, the more comfortable you'll be with the next step and the one after that. You don't need a running start. Just go.

- Try the second method, too. Pick some personality trait or quality that you'd love to see yourself have. At the earliest opportunity, just be that. React in the way a person with that characteristic would react. If you want to be more loving, behave in a loving way. If you want to be braver or more confident, act the way a brave or confident person acts.

- Don't worry that people will think your transformation is abrupt. You don't have to include extra steps just to show your work. You were that, now you're this. And now you're still this from now on. Try it. You might prefer this method. (I do.)

24

WHAT IF YOUR TIME IS FOR YOU?

Do you treat yourself as if you don't deserve your own time? Do other people get to waste your time when you'd rather spend it on you?

I sometimes teach women's self-defense classes at the dorms of my local university along with another black belt friend of mine, Michele. We love it. It's so exciting to see young college women gain so much confidence in just the course of an evening.

Michele always asks whether any of them use the on-campus safety escorts when they're leaving the library or a late class to return to their dorms at night. Few of them do, even though they know about the service and it's free. And most give the same reason: "It takes too long. I don't want to have to wait."

We understand that. We also understand why some of

them are embarrassed about the idea of asking—as if that makes them weak somehow.

But we tell them it's the opposite: Taking proper care of themselves is a strong, confident move, and it's always a good use of their own time.

I had my own epiphany about this several years ago when I read an article about the habit a lot of women have of holding our pee. You know what I'm talking about. We're so busy, we'll get to it in a minute, let me just finish these phone calls, I'm right in the middle of something … and an hour later you're still holding it.

Why? Aren't you important enough to yourself to make your own comfort a priority? Can't you spare a few minutes when you need it? After reading that article I realized that peeing when I needed to was such a simple, easy kindness to pay to myself. And it turned out to be just the first step toward other small kindnesses: Not wearing clothes that hurt. Adding padding to a backpack strap that was chafing. Stopping to shake a pebble out of my shoe instead of just putting up with it. Getting a drink of water when I was thirsty—all small acts of friendship to myself that were worth my own time and effort.

And aside from these issues of safety and comfort, there's the overall question of whether we allow ourselves to enjoy our time here on earth every day in all sorts of ways. Do you take the time to read if that's what you love? Do you take the time to look at art or listen to music? Or to exercise if you know that would feel good? Do you take time to do nothing, to just sit in a chair with your eyes closed and let your thoughts have a little quiet time to settle?

Or do you let other people interfere with your serenity by jabbering at you night and day?

There's a difference between wasting time and spending it. Talking to a friend whose conversation you value is spending time. Listening to someone complain or gossip or just monologue for an hour without ever asking you a single question about yourself—that person is wasting your time. And you don't have to allow it.

We all have only exactly twenty-four hours at our disposal every day. Some of that time is for sleeping. Some is for work. Some is for daily obligations, some of it is for our Uses, and some of it is for fun. Remember fun? Do you wonder sometimes why you don't play more, laugh more, and just plain *relax*? Maybe it's because the time you have to do all of those things is being steadily stolen away by people who aren't adding value and happiness to your life.

Try doing it a different way. "I only have five minutes, then I have to go." Stick to the five minutes and end your call. "Ohh, I was just on my way out. We'll have to catch up later." Cheerfully end the call. If it's not a phone call, but face to face, "I was just about to call my mother/my accountant/someone I'm doing a project with that's due tomorrow. They've been waiting for me. Can we talk later?" And then maybe "later" never comes. If you've given yourself an out, take it. If you decide to call or meet the person later and subject yourself to a stream of words you don't care about and that fray your nerves—maybe you'll make a different choice next time.

We get into the habit of giving away our time and attention to anyone who wants it. We don't want to seem rude. We like to be nice. But nice means nice to you, too. Fair includes fair to you. If you've been craving that hour to yourself to just slow down and be quiet and let your thoughts finally catch up with you, don't give away your precious time to someone else instead. They might benefit from the quiet, too, but that's up to them. How you spend your own free time really is your choice. Find out how nice it feels to finally pick you.

- Today notice the times you force yourself to wait when you shouldn't have to. Are you holding your pee? Are you hungry and not taking time to feed yourself? Are you tired and not giving yourself rest? If you don't take care of yourself in these small, daily ways, who will?

- When you take the time to address some physical need, you are showing yourself that you matter. When you let other people wait while you eat something or use the restroom or take the time to breathe some fresh air, you're reminding yourself and them that you place a high value on your own health and your calm clear mind. What we see ourselves do tells us who we are. You are always worth your own time. Let yourself see that.

25

WHAT IF YOUR MONEY IS FOR YOU?

Is it hard for you to say no when someone you are close to wants or needs money from you? We all like to feel generous, especially when we have more resources than someone else, but can that impulse toward generosity become a burden? When is it all right—and more than that, when is it *essential*—to start preserving your money for your own important uses?

When I was a lawyer, I took business courses every now and then on managing the financial aspect of owning a law firm. Because believe it or not, lawyers can sometimes be really bad at collecting their own fees from their clients. I know one law firm that constantly carries millions on its accounts receivable ledger. Even though the lawyers have done the work, the clients just don't pay.

As you might imagine, that leads to a lot of resentment. Because lawyers are often ethically bound to continue working on certain cases, even if the client stops paying. It's not like an automated car wash, one lawyer told me. He can't just stop spraying when the quarters are used up.

One of the seminars I went to discussed the psychological effects of not being paid. And the presenter made an interesting distinction: When we do work for free *on purpose* (also known as *pro bono* work), we feel good about ourselves. Because it's our choice. But when we do work for free because someone has stiffed us, we feel angry and used.

The same thing applies in our personal lives. When we give money to a charity or treat our friends to lunch for their birthdays, we feel good about the transaction. We meant to give that gift.

But when a friend or family member is constantly hitting us up for money or in some other way draining our own resources because of certain choices they've made—not you, but them—we often feel resentful and angry, but don't really feel right about saying no.

Give yourself permission to say no.

You have important things to do with your life. And a lot of those things require money. You need to be financially healthy and independent so you have the freedom to pursue your own dreams and desires.

When you put your own financial picture first, you see how you want to pay off debt, accumulate savings, have money not only for the monthly necessities, but also for the occasional sweet expenditures you're entitled to just to make yourself happy. You have a list of things you want to do, maybe classes you want to take, experiences you want to enjoy.

And money makes all of those possible.

But when other people continue to make choices for their own lives that result in constant financial crises—crises they look to you to fix, because you're so nice and also you have more money than they do, so isn't it fair, and it doesn't really hurt you, etc.—then you're only delaying that day when they realize they need to change what they're doing and clean up their own situation.

It's also worth noticing the things those people *do* have money for: in some cases drugs or alcohol, money for gambling, money for frivolous things that you don't buy yourself because you're more responsible with your resources. And every time you have to bail someone out, you get more and more resentful because you wouldn't live your life that way, so why do you have to keep paying for someone else's willful or simply foolish mistakes?

Well, you don't. Here are some strategies for helping you say no, even when it's difficult:

1. Honestly tie up your money in *you*. It's helpful to think of an extreme case to realize it's okay to do this without having the worst happen to you. What if your house burned down? Or you were in an accident and had hundreds of thousands of dollars in medical bills, and were also out of work for two years? What if you found out you had a deadly illness and needed to go to a special hospital in Switzerland right away? Or to be more positive, what if

you decided you wanted to send yourself to college or graduate school?

Wouldn't you feel fine in any of those situations about gathering in all your money and using it for yourself, without any guilt about not letting other people drain it away? Of course you would. Because you matter. Your life and health and physical needs matter. Your education and career matter. You could sincerely say, "I'm sorry, but I need all of my money for myself right now. You're going to have to figure out something else."

Well, guess what? Your life does matter—*right now*. Without having the worst happen to you or without deciding you have to go to med school just to have a good reason to keep your money to yourself.

What are the things you want to learn and do right now? Are there classes you want to take, crafts you want to learn, books you want to buy? Those are important expenses—as much as a car loan and rent and everything else in your budget. Because **your life matters**. It seems so easy to forget that, especially when we're faced with having to say no to someone we care about.

I won't pretend it's easy to say no the first few times. But this does make it easier: Every time someone asks you for money, run it through this filter in your own mind. Ask yourself, "If my house had just burned down, or I'd just lost everything because of some horrible accident or disease, would I want to give money to this person instead of using it to take care of myself?" You can even use the same response that you would then: "I'm sorry, but I have some situations in my own life right now. I don't have any extra money I can spare."

And it's true: the "situations" are your own happiness and financial security. You don't have to say that, but just know it in your heart and stand firm in taking care of yourself.

2. Realize that something of value you can give to people other than money is a demonstration of what a financially secure and healthy lifestyle looks like. Do they want what you have? Great—show them or tell them how to get it. Be their inspiration. That's a more lasting gift than constantly handing over hundreds of dollars to bail someone out of yet another financial crisis.

I once did this for a friend of mine who trusted me enough to let me install a bookkeeping program on his computer and input a whole year of his bank statements so he could finally see his financial situation. Up until then, he never balanced his checkbook or kept track of his spending, which meant that he was constantly having checks bounce and incurring bank fees for being overdrawn on his debit and credit cards. A real mess. But instead of giving him the thousands he needed to clean it up, I spent an entire Saturday helping him get his financial information organized. He would have preferred the cash at the time, but I wasn't willing to give it. My act of love was giving him my time and knowledge. And that was a far better gift for him in the long run.

3. Develop your no and stick to it. Practice it and be strong. "I know you want money, and I can't give it right

now." Without apology. If you're not comfortable saying only that much, you can even add something like, "I have a ton of expenses right now. I have to take care of a lot of stuff." You don't have to say what that stuff is, even if the person asks. It's your business how you spend your money. And you've decided to spend it on your own life. You're entitled. Believe it.

This is one of those topics that is so fraught with emotion because we want to be kind to the people we love. But that *must* include yourself! **You matter**. No one will ever care about you as much as you care about yourself. So please be kind and loving to yourself today, and decide that your financial security is one of the most important gifts you can give to you.

- Today notice how you feel as you spend money on different things. Write to yourself about it. Ask yourself questions. Is there a difference between how you feel when you donate money to a charity or spend it on a gift for someone you love, versus spending it because of some obligation? That obligation might include paying your regular bills or supporting someone you feel duty-bound to support. Then think of a third category: Items you pay for because you want or need them and know they cost money. Do you spend money cheerfully in those instances, or do you resent what the things you want cost?

- All of these are choices. Even paying your bills is a choice. If you want the electricity to remain on or your car to remain yours, you choose to pay those bills. But so much of our spending can be unconscious. We're out of money at the end of every month and aren't sure why. Today notice how you spend your money and how each expenditure feels to you. Which ones are worth it? Which ones are not? If some of your habitual expenditures no longer provide value to you in exchange, can you decide for yourself that it's time to let them go?

26

WHAT IF YOU WANT TO PURSUE YOUR DREAM?

No matter how far out of reach a particular dream might seem from where you are now, you know there are *steps*. Whether you're willing to put in the effort to take those steps is up to you. But there's great comfort in knowing that you could use your intelligence to do the research and write down a list of a hundred—maybe even a *thousand*—small steps that you could begin taking today.

A long time ago I started keeping a Life List: writing down everything I wanted to learn and know and try, and adding to it all the time. I broke it down into four categories: Skills I Want to Learn (like becoming fluent in a particular language and learning to ride a horse); Places I Want to Go (Scotland, Newfoundland, New Zealand—lots of "lands"); Experiences I Want to Have (making fire from scratch, galloping on a horse without being afraid, etc.);

and Creative Projects I Want to Pursue (writing certain books, writing screenplays, etc.).

What's great about a comprehensive list like that is I have so many choices all the time. It means there's always *something* I can do. Because every single item on that list has steps. Going to New Zealand, for example: research plane fare, do research online about places in the country to visit, figure out the right time of year, and so on. Those steps matter. They're necessary. And they're easy. Accomplishing even the small, simple steps makes me feel like, "Okay, I can do this. Keep going."

I love to help other people accomplish their dreams. It's one of my Uses. I'm also aware that it's my number one way of diverting time and energy away from my own projects. Who can resist sitting down with a friend on a Saturday, both of you with fresh new pads of paper, and spending the next several hours making lists all of the steps to accomplish something new? The trick I've had to learn is how to let my friends then go off to their own lives and take all the steps themselves. I've stopped volunteering to do half of them just to help get their dreams off the ground.

Whatever dream it is you want to pursue, there's a way to break it down into small, manageable bits. The more simple, easily-doable parts you can list, the more items you get to check off. Also, the smaller the steps, the less nervous some people are about finally moving toward an unfamiliar path.

You want to sell your artwork online? Great! I could do

a whole Saturday list for that, but so can you. You want to become a dolphin trainer? That sounds amazing! Here, let me set aside my project and help you.

1. Search online for video about dolphin training.
2. Watch video (or more likely, watch 10 videos in a row).
3. Search for books about dolphin training.
4. Get one book.
5. Read one book. (Then keep adding books.)
6. Research degree/education dolphin trainers need.
7. Research places offering that degree/education.
8. Research scholarships for degree/education.

Trust me, I could go on and on.

Each of the items on that list is something you could do right away, today. If someone expected you to be training their dolphin tomorrow, you'd have to tell them to wait. But you'd already be on your way toward that goal just by completing your smaller steps.

Whatever your dreams are, they are yours for a reason. Your life matters. Your Uses matter. What you feel drawn to do is important. So if there is something you truly want to do in your life, go ahead and make your list. Then start moving. Do one thing at a time, and do one of those things today. A day from now you'll already be a whole day further down the road. And maybe that's all you need to keep yourself going.

- Today make your list. Or make several lists, like I did with my own Life List. Start asking yourself all of the many things you want to do with your life, and then take your answers seriously. Is it crazy to say you want to be a dolphin trainer? Some people **are** dolphin trainers. Is it unrealistic to think you can become an opera singer when you've never received any training? I don't know. I'd have to research it. That would probably be the first item on my list. But I'd still make a full list. In fact, I'm already thinking of it now…

- Select one or two items from the beginning of your list and do them right away. Set a goal for yourself of checking off at least one item a day. If you're serious, and you really want this, you'll show that to yourself by how seriously you move down your list. If you believe it will take years to accomplish, it probably will. If you believe you can do it more quickly, you're probably right. Your dreams wait on you.

27

WHAT IF YOU'RE NOT TOO LATE?

We tell ourselves such interesting things to keep from pursuing our paths. It's too soon. It isn't the right time yet. It's too late. I'm too old. I've lost my chance. I'm already too far behind.

What if none of that is actually true?

It's never the perfect time. There will always be reasons why you should hold off a little longer, do more research, lose a little more weight first, set aside more money—whatever the hold up is, once you've got *that* done, then you can start living your bigger life.

And yet, it's always the perfect time. Because the truth is—and you've seen this in action just like I have—if you keep waiting, you'll just have to have this same conversation with yourself a few weeks or months or even years from now.

Whereas if you started *now*, today, even taking just a

step or two in the direction you intend to go, by tomorrow you'll already be that much further into it. And then do it again the next day and the next, and pretty soon you can look back at a stretch of trail and think, *Yeah, I did that. I can do this.*

I used to own a business with a friend of mine from law school. He and I were and are great buddies, and I felt an obligation to him to keep going with the business even when I knew I was burnt out on it.

So every day I'd take steps toward what I really wanted —to be a full-time writer—but then I'd spend the evening doing work on our business and not enjoying it one bit.

But I was afraid to tell him. I didn't want to leave him in the lurch. I was the primary operator of the business, and if I quit, the business would go away.

Then I spent some time one afternoon just sitting quietly with myself and picturing what I was doing. What I saw was this: Every day I hiked up a beautiful mountainside and moved further up my trail, but then by nightfall I'd run back down the mountain to where my friend had his camp. Then the next morning I'd have to regain all that same ground as I hiked upward again.

So I told him. And he was fine with it. Turns out he was tired of it, too, and everything worked out.

But what I realized is that I could have spared myself a lot of angst by having that conversation months before, instead of waiting for whatever that "perfect" time was going to be. There was no perfect time. There was just the time when I finally did it.

What if you're concerned that it's already too late to pursue your dream—that the time for that has passed and now you're too old?

I'll never forget a Dear Abby advice column I read back when I was a teenager. A woman wrote in that she wanted to go to medical school and become a doctor, but she was already in her thirties. "By the time I'm done, I'll be forty." Abby's answer? "You'll be forty anyway, so why not do what you want?"

The same applies no matter what age you are. The funny thing is, I've heard it from both sides: "I'm only fifteen! How can I..." "I'm already seventy! How can I..." The answer is, *You're alive, aren't you? So go live!* You're going to be a day older by the end of today anyway, so why not do what you want?

And if you're unsure of how long it might take you and whether you'll be able to accomplish what you set out to do, just look back on your life up to now—even just the last ten years. Haven't you already come so far and changed so much in that time? Why should your life be any different in the next ten years?

What if the issue isn't your age, but the fact that you're already so far behind? That if you really wanted to pursue your dream, you should have started months or years ago? Now there are so many other people doing what you wanted to do, they're all so much further along than you are, and you still have so much to do before you can catch up. Isn't it too late?

I once accompanied the daughter of a friend of mine to

a meeting with her college advisor. Elise was in trouble. It was the end of her freshman year, and for the second semester in a row she'd gotten dismal grades. On top of that, she'd just received a letter saying she was on academic probation. Dark days indeed. She felt like she was in a hole too deep to climb out of. Her dream of pursuing a college degree was slipping out of her hands.

The advisor explained how Elise could mend the problem by retaking one of the core classes. "But my parents will be so mad!" she told him. "If I retake it, I'll be so far behind!"

He looked at her like he didn't even understand the concept. "There is no behind. You're just progressing. This is college. You're doing it."

And with that, all of the tension left the room and Elise could actually relax for the first time in weeks. Because he was right. She was just progressing. There was no point in regretting every single choice that had put her there. These were the facts, this was reality, and all she could do was go forward. And do better from then on.

I have thought of that conversation *so* many times since then—specifically every time I'm rushing some project or feeling internal pressure because I haven't met some goal or deadline, usually one I've set up for myself. I'm constantly reminding myself now, "There is no behind. You're just progressing." It applies to finishing my books, getting chores done, sorting out my schedule and my finances and whatever else crops up from day to day. And just saying that to myself, out loud, gives me the same calm it did that day in the advisor's office.

What if it's not too late? What if you're not behind? What if it isn't too soon? What if you're not too old? What if you stopped telling yourself any of that, and instead simply kept progressing along your path?

You don't have to wait anymore. Today is a fine day to set out on your new stretch of trail. It looks like the perfect weather for it, you're all ready to go, and you don't need to wait for anyone else's permission or blessing. Just walk. Pull on your boots and hike.

And then hang on to all that fresh mileage you gain today, and resist the temptation to run back down the hill.

- Today look at some deadline you've set for yourself. Is it real, or just a preference? Can you be flexible and change it? If you have some personal deadline in mind and you know you're not going to meet it, but you can see that you're moving forward steadily every day, what more can you do? Let go of your deadline. Continue progressing. You're not in trouble and you're not behind.

28

WHAT IF YOU AIM PAST YOUR TARGETS?

Think about your various goals. Are they achievable? That's good, but are they *too* achievable? Too easy? Could you push yourself a little past what seems like a comfortable goal, and aim for something bigger?

Sometimes the honest answer is no, we're too afraid. We might be holding back on thinking bigger because ... what if we really get it?

In martial arts training we learn how to punch and kick with power. If we're going to do either, we want the impact to count. To practice, our training partner holds a pad in front of us, and then we aim at least six inches beyond that target when we strike. Why?

If we aim only as far as the pad, our power will start tailing off too early. But if the true target is some distance beyond the pad, then look out. **POW**.

It's the same for runners in a race: If they aim only as

far as the finish line, their bodies start subtly losing momentum in those last few precious seconds. But if they aim past the finish line, even if it's just a foot or two beyond it, their momentum carries them through.

My friend Pete likes to sit down with himself twice a year, on New Year's Eve and his birthday (which happen to be about six months apart), and have a chat with himself about what he would like to accomplish during the next half of the year. That much of it sounds like a fairly common planning exercise.

What isn't common is that Pete imagines himself as he wants to be six months ahead, and it's that version of himself who runs the meeting with his current, six-month's-younger self.

As his future self, he gives his current self "marching orders," as he calls them, of what to do in these next six months so that he can be, do, and have what he wants by then.

I think it's a wonderful way of doing it. I've tried it myself and I love it.

Last time we compared our experiences with his method, Pete confessed that he was having what he thought was a strange problem: He could feel himself resisting how good things could be. "I see a potential future," he said, "I know it's possible, but … it just seems *too* good. I'm not always sure I'm ready."

I get that. A lot of us seem to have an internal set-point of how much good we're willing to believe can really come to us in our lives. And another set-point for how successful we can be and how much we can accomplish in the world.

But rather than limit ourselves, the better response is to reset those set-points a lot higher and finally drop once and for all any lingering fear that what we're asking of our lives might be too good. It's all right, we're allowed to do great things. It's what we're all here for. The only ones who have made up rules about how small our lives need to be are us. And so the good news is that we ourselves have the power to fix that.

Don't hold back. If the possibilities for your life seem too big and too good, be grateful that you are who you are and gladly accept them. Maybe some of your Uses in this world can benefit from a certain level of success. If it makes you more comfortable, think larger with that in mind.

- Today try Pete's exercise. You don't have to wait for New Year's or your birthday or some other significant event, today is significant enough.

- See yourself as the person you'd most love to be by some particular date or age. Then start asking questions: How did you become this? What steps did you take? What things make you happiest in your life right now? How did you get those? How do you feel about yourself? What advice do you have for me, your younger self? What beliefs do I need to have about myself so that I can have the confidence to become you? Once you start, you'll think of plenty of questions of your own.

29

WHAT IF NOT SHARING WHO YOU ARE DEPRIVES THE WORLD OF A GIFT?

Not everyone feels confident going boldly out into the world and telling everyone what he or she has to offer. Maybe you've invented something new. Maybe you know vast amounts about a specialized topic. Maybe you have some talent as a painter or musician or actress, but it's a talent you're still wondering whether anyone will want to see or hear.

You're looking at it the wrong way. You're only thinking of yourself. Put yourself in other people's shoes: If you've invented something that can bring comfort or convenience to their lives, would they be worse off if they never had it? If people knew what you could teach them, would they feel sad that they never learned? And if your talent in the arts could bring joy or inspiration or entertainment to someone after a long and difficult day, wouldn't that person's life feel thinner and less rich for not being able to experience what you can do?

I think about how I feel as a consumer myself, especially of books: I love it when someone has written something that uplifts me or teaches me something new. I appreciate that the author went to the trouble of writing about his or her experiences and knowledge so that I can skip over a lot of mistakes and missteps and do something better.

And sometimes I don't even know that I want to learn a particular thing until I see someone offering to teach it. Then yes, you bet I'd love to learn how to sketch with watercolor or bake sourdough bread from scratch or how to fix a broken leg with materials I scrounge from the woods.

What might you be depriving me and all the rest of the world of by being shy about telling us what you know? Have you been so caught up in thinking *"No one could possibly want to hear me talk/write about X"* that you've forgotten to let *us* be the judge of that? What else are you holding back? Won't you show us so we can see if we want it?

It reminds me of a writing teacher I had who cautioned us not to be so critical of our own work that we never sent it out. "Don't pre-reject yourself," he said. "Give other people the chance to decide for themselves if they like it. Because maybe they *will*, and they never would have known that if you kept revising and putting it back in your drawer and being too afraid to share it."

It's such excellent advice. And something I've had to remind myself over the years as certain projects felt too risky or different for me to publish. But do you know what? The two books that I was most nervous about sharing with the world have been my two biggest sellers. I'm glad I didn't pre-reject them.

My friend Rebecca loves to take photographs. One day she decided to stop keeping them to herself, and instead uploaded them to the various sites where people can buy stock footage. Now every time someone buys one of her photographs, Rebecca feels *great*. Because not only has she made a little money from her art, she also knows she took a photo that someone can use—a photo of a remote, beautiful place that most people won't have the time or opportunity to visit themselves. She has added value to someone else's life. Fantastic.

So think about it today: What gift have you been keeping under wraps that the rest of us would feel so happy to get from you? Don't think about yourself and how shy or nervous you might be about sharing it, think about all of *us*. You provide a valuable service by not pre-rejecting your product or service or art, and instead letting it find the people who want what you have to give.

- Today pay attention to all of the products and services in your life that you appreciate someone else for creating. Not only creating, but then sharing with the world so that now you get to enjoy it. How many things do you cheerfully buy each day that other people thought to invent? What if they had kept their wonderful gifts to themselves? Wouldn't you miss the usefulness, convenience, or artistry of what they made? Think about the equation from their side: How much bravery did it take to share what they could do? Aren't you so grateful they did?

- What gift *have* you been keeping under wraps? Is it something you've written? Something you've made? Some knowledge or experience you have that you can teach? A product or service you have to offer? More than likely, you have more than one thing. Finish it. Offer it. Share it. Sell it. Put it out where we can see it and enjoy it and use it. Think about us on this side of the equation, the people whose lives you'll add value to if you just call upon your bravery.

30

WHAT IF YOU'RE READY TO GO FOR IT?

You're ready. You know it. At least you *think* you know it. You're about to make a change in your life or pursue one of your dreams. But there are still those few nagging doubts that make you wonder if you're right. What if no one really wants what you have to offer? What if isn't good enough? What if you've just fooled yourself into thinking you can make a go of what you want?

We all know about the "glass half-full" versus "glass half-empty" distinction. But my husband and I had our own variation. Back before I sold my first novel to a publisher, we used to go to one of the big chain bookstores every now and then, and we'd leave with different perspectives.

He'd say, "Wow, there are so many books out there already. How will you ever sell yours?"

Whereas I'd come away thinking, "Wow! Look at all

those books that get published all the time! Mine has a good chance, too!"

This isn't a complaint about my husband, whom I love, it's an observation about belief and optimism and moving forward toward a dream.

Maybe you're like me, and there are only a few people in your immediate circle who actually understand some of the creative or other dreams you have for your life. I'm fortunate that one of my brothers is a professional musician and composer, and my best friend is talented in a wide array of artistic pursuits. Both of them understand the thrill of creating something new that never existed before.

Not only do we understand each other, but we believe in each other's paths to a career in the arts—whereas a lot of my friends from my law and business days have a little more trouble. When I tell them I'm working on a new screenplay, it probably sounds as realistic to them as if I said I decided to try out for the NFL just as soon as I've finished building an enclosure for my pet whale.

But I always know that if I want something, I actually have to do the steps. You know it, too. My follow-up thought after looking around in the chock-full bookstore was always, "A hundred percent of the books in here were written first." It motivated me to go back home and continue writing.

Are you there yet? Are you ready? No running start needed, just the confident next step, and now you're already on the path you imagined. How does it feel? Daunting? Exhilarating? Not sure yet? Keep walking.

But what if you're *almost* there, and you can see the path, but you can't seem to compel yourself forward anymore? Is there something you've been holding back from starting or completing or putting out there into the world? Why? What is the true reason? What is your specific fear?

Are you afraid of exposure, of people seeing some private talent or Use of yours that you aren't sure you feel ready to share? Are you afraid things might start to get *too good*? Are you worried that if you actually commit to this dream and go for it, and it doesn't work out the way you hoped, you'll have nothing to look forward to anymore?

I understand all of these fears and more. I'm one of the many, *many* people who resisted my own joy and true Uses for longer than I can now believe. Why didn't I do what I wanted when I first knew what it was? I've dreamed of being a writer since I was in fifth grade. So why did I go to law school instead? Then later, when I quit lawyering, why did I start my own business instead? I wasn't confused. I knew what was in my heart. But I was afraid and there's no other reason I can give. I simply lacked the courage.

But I will give you this secret, because it was one of the reasons I finally came around. It's the same reason I was always excited by what I saw in the giant bookstore: **If someone else has done it, it means that I can, too.** Even if someone hasn't done the *specific* thing I want to do, I know from all the many biographies I read that people throughout history, all with their own wide variety of skills and talents and Uses, have gotten ideas into their heads and then set off to do the things they imagined.

We can do that, too. I'm smart, you're smart, we know things. We're willing to break our dreams into small, achievable steps and then actually go take those steps in a persistent, purposeful way.

How do I know that about you? Because you have read to nearly the end of this book. If you didn't believe you could get the most out of your life, you would have lost interest already and gone off and done something else with your time. Instead, you've kept reading.

Remember that one hundred percent of the books that have been published were first written. Apply that formula to whatever you've decided to go after, and confidently do your work. *Finishing* things already puts you far ahead of all those people who just talk about it or start but never see it through.

Have courage. Have faith in yourself. **GO FOR IT**.

- Are you still holding back and you're not exactly sure why? Write to yourself. Ask yourself questions. Ask again. Be kind and gentle with yourself. This isn't a time for scolding. You're not in trouble. Find out what fears you have that tell you it's not safe to do what you want to do. Is it fear about what your family and friends will say? About how you'll support yourself? About whether moving to a new location or changing your work would mean you'd lose whatever security you now have?

- There are no set answers to whatever questions you might have. You are your best counselor. You know what you need to say and hear and do. So give yourself time until pursuing your dream feels like exactly the right next move. And once it is, GO.

31

WHAT IF YOU'RE DOING IT RIGHT?

Consider that if you're good at something and you love it, you should do it.

We are born with certain traits: our eye color; the length of our index fingers versus the middle one (look around—people are different); whether we can curl our tongues, easily read music, draw, run fast, do complicated calculations in our head; maybe it's a love for helping people, or an affinity with animals—whatever it is, it's yours. So many talents and interests in this world, and no one has the exact same combination as you do.

You know you are unique. You can try to hide it, try to blend in with the crowd, but in your heart you know that you are the only you.

Have faith in who you are. Have faith that who you are is deliberate. That your life and your passions and your personality are what they're supposed to be.

So one day soon when you give yourself the time to write down all the things you're good at, and mix it with all the things you're interested in, and add in those elements that make you excited to get up in the morning and keep you staying up past exhaustion because you're not ready to stop, you love it so much—

Maybe that's the thing. Have faith. Try it.

And when you do, know that you're also helping other people around you who are looking to you as an example. You may not know it, but they're there.

It's exciting to see someone who is real. Don't you love to read an interview with someone famous and find out that he or she thinks the same way you do about things and goes through the same doubts and struggles?

And yet still they pursue their passions with persistence because it's what they want to do and they believe they can do it.

It's inspiring. It shows the rest of us what we can do, too. And now is the time to understand and take pleasure from the fact that you are also an inspiration to others.

When you have doubts, when your path isn't as easy as you wanted, when you wonder whether you should keep going or just give up and go back to being ordinary—think of the people following behind. Think of that one person—or perhaps thousands and thousands of people—out there whom you might never meet, who will one day want to retrace how you got to be who you are.

You inspire your friends by being real. You inspire people you come into contact with every day by being kind and thoughtful and also by standing up for yourself and saying what you want. You can't know now what qualities of yours someone else desperately needs to see in action, but trust that whenever you are living as yourself, you are showing the world what can be done.

Keep going. Life wants you. Exactly you. You're doing it right.

- Today put aside your fears and doubts for the entire day, and live as if you already know that all of your plans and dreams will work out. You can pick up your fears again tomorrow, but for today they'll have to wait.

- How differently do you think and speak and act when you already know that what you want is yours? That you already are the person you intended to be, back when you began shedding those extra layers of other people's expectations that you realized you didn't need anymore? How confident does your voice sound? How happy do you feel? How do you carry your body? What words do you say about yourself?

- You can reverse-engineer your life. Just like my friend Pete having a conference with his future self, you can begin where you want to be and work backwards. Meet the current you somewhere along your path. You might be years apart from each other right now, or only a few days. Have faith in that future. Have faith in yourself. Hold your picture of the life you want always in your mind and keep taking all the steps to arrive there. Hold your vision of yourself and keep walking forward to meet you.

THANK YOU FOR READING. This book is from my heart to yours. I wish you all the best.

ABOUT THE AUTHOR

Robin Brande is an award-winning author, former trial attorney, black belt in martial arts, Reiki Master, and wilderness medic. Her outdoor adventures range from the Rocky Mountains to the Alps to Iceland.

She writes in multiple genres, including mystery, adventure, fantasy, science fiction, young adult, romance, and self-help.

For more information:
https://robinbrande.com/

For information about new releases, along with special discounts on books and merchandise, subscribe to the Robin Brande newsletter: https://robinbrande.com/pages/subscribe.

www.ingramcontent.com/pod-product-compliance
Lightning Source LLC
Chambersburg PA
CBHW030152100526
44592CB00009B/239